The CELTIC CROSS TAROT SPREAD

Cutting to the Chase

Shannon MacLeod
Illustrations by Beth Seilonen

Schiffer Publishing Ltd
4880 Lower Valley Road • Atglen, PA 19310

Other Schiffer Tarot decks by Shannon MacLeod (writing as Jennifer ShadowFox):
ShadowFox Tarot 978-0-7643-3487-0

Other Schiffer Tarot Decks by Beth Seilonen:
Tarot Leaves 978-0-7643-3903-5
Dream Raven Tarot 978-0-7643-4316-2
Bleu Cat Tarot 978-0-7643-4553-1

Copyright © 2014 by Shannon MacLeod
Illustrations © 2014 Beth Seilonen

Library of Congress Control Number: 2014940502

All rights reserved. No part of this work may be reproduced or used in any form or by any means—graphic, electronic, or mechanical, including photocopying or information storage and retrieval systems—without written permission from the publisher.
The scanning, uploading and distribution of this book or any part thereof via the Internet or via any other means without the permission of the publisher is illegal and punishable by law. Please purchase only authorized editions and do not participate in or encourage the electronic piracy of copyrighted materials.
"Schiffer," "Schiffer Publishing, Ltd. & Design," and the "Design of pen and inkwell" are registered trademarks of Schiffer Publishing, Ltd.

Type set in MeyerTwo/Book Antiqua

ISBN: 978-0-7643-4588-3
Printed in The United States

Schiffer Books are available at special discounts for bulk purchases for sales promotions or premiums. Special editions, including personalized covers, corporate imprints, and excerpts can be created in large quantities for special needs. For more information contact the publisher:

Published by Schiffer Publishing, Ltd.
4880 Lower Valley Road
Atglen, PA 19310
Phone: (610) 593-1777; Fax: (610) 593-2002
E-mail: Info@schifferbooks.com

For the largest selection of fine reference books on this and related subjects, please visit our website at **www.schifferbooks.com**.
We are always looking for people to write books on new and related subjects. If you have an idea for a book, please contact us at proposals@schifferbooks.com

This book may be purchased from the publisher.
Please try your bookstore first.
You may write for a free catalog.

Dedication

To Taylor and Nolan,
the two halves of my heart

Acknowledgments

To Angela, my silver bird – keeper of lore and secrets, baker of gendered fudge, and the most vicious gamer in the known world.
(Don't ask her about the balloon. EVER).

To Dinah, my wonderful editor who believed in me when no one else did.

To Tricia, my voice of reason who moonlights as a pixie (her dust is in her other purse) – artist, muse, arranger of words and hooper to the max.

To Richard and Virginia, who love me anyway.

To Mermaid Jones – long may she swim wild and free.

And last but not least –

To ET, who gave me Cups and Wands when the world gave me Swords.

Contents

Foreword	6
How to Use This Book	7
The Celtic Cross	8
The Three-Card Reading	11
The One-Card Reading	12
The Tarot Cards	15
The Majors	16
0. The Fool	17
1. The Magician	20
2. The High Priestess	23
3. The Empress	26
4. The Emperor	29
5. The Hierophant	32
6. The Lovers	35
7. The Chariot	38
8. Strength	41
9. The Hermit	44
10. The Wheel of Fortune	47
11. Justice	50
12. The Hanged Man	53
13. Death	56
14. Temperance	59
15. The Devil	62
16. The Tower	65
17. The Star	68
18. The Moon	71
19. The Sun	74
20. Judgment	77
21. The World	80

The Minors	83
Swords	84
The Ace of Swords	85
The Two of Swords	88
The Three of Swords	90
The Four of Swords	92
The Five of Swords	94
The Six of Swords	96
The Seven of Swords	98
The Eight of Swords	100
The Nine of Swords	102
The Ten of Swords	104
Wands	106
The Ace of Wands	107
The Two of Wands	109
The Three of Wands	111
The Four of Wands	113
The Five of Wands	115
The Six of Wands	117
The Seven of Wands	119
The Eight of Wands	121
The Nine of Wands	123
The Ten of Wands	125

Cups	**127**
The Ace of Cups	128
The Two of Cups	130
The Three of Cups	132
The Four of Cups	134
The Five of Cups	136
The Six of Cups	138
The Seven of Cups	140
The Eight of Cups	142
The Nine of Cups	144
The Ten of Cups	146
Pentacles	**148**
The Ace of Pentacles	149
The Two of Pentacles	151
The Three of Pentacles	153
The Four of Pentacles	155
The Five of Pentacles	157
The Six of Pentacles	159
The Seven of Pentacles	161
The Eight of Pentacles	163
The Nine of Pentacles	165
The Ten of Pentacles	167

The Tarot Court	**169**
Swords	**171**
The Page of Swords	172
The Knight of Swords	174
The Queen of Swords	176
The King of Swords	178
Wands	**180**
The Page of Wands	181
The Knight of Wands	183
The Queen of Wands	185
The King of Wands	187
Cups	**189**
The Page of Cups	190
The Knight of Cups	192
The Queen of Cups	194
The King of Cups	196
Pentacles	**198**
The Page of Pentacles	199
The Knight of Pentacles	201
The Queen of Pentacles	203
The King of Pentacles	205
Conclusion	**207**

Foreword

So you're interested in learning to read the Tarot?

Put this book down now and walk away — this is not the one you seek. Look around and see if you can find something by Mary Kay Greer, Rachel Pollack, Robert Place, or Lon Milo DuQuette instead.

So you're interested in reading the Tarot but don't have the time/patience/desire to do all the studying and memorization required? Draw up a chair, darling. Sit by me and let me tell you the story of how all this came about. The idea came from my then thirteen-year-old daughter who requested a Tarot reading to give her deeper insight on (insert most recent teenage drama here). The conversation went something like this:

Her: "So will you do a reading for me?"

Me: *sighs* "Why don't you learn to do it yourself? I can teach you…"

Her: "Because there are 78 cards and upright and reversed and different meanings depending on what the position is and that's a lot to remember and WHY CAN'T YOU JUST TELL ME WHAT IT MEANS?"

The last part ended in a particularly piercing wail and I acquiesced just to make it stop. Hence, the book you're holding now, so that you, too, can "just find out what it means." Enjoy!

How to Use This Book

It's not hard. There are hundreds of different spreads, or ways to lay out the cards. We're only going to focus on three: the Celtic (hard C as in "Keltic" — we're not talking about a basketball team, after all) Cross which uses ten cards, a three-card spread and a one-card. I'm going to tell you what pattern to lay the cards in, you look up the positions and *BAM!* Instant Tarot reading — easy peasy.

It's not all cruise control on your part, though — there's a tiny bit of work involved. Bear in mind that upright is the card facing you, reversed means it's upside down. When you look up a card's positional meaning, try to get the general feeling of what is written. Try it on, play with it — make it your own. Make the concept of the prompt fit your question. For example, this section from The Emperor:

> The need for cooler heads and logical thinking prevails. There may be a need for someone to step up and assume leadership to right the helm of a listing ship — you, perhaps?

The key words/phrases in this sentence are cooler heads, logical thinking, assume leadership. If you pull this card in the second position, it tells you these are the qualities you need to do battle with (the current drama). See how it works?

Any Tarot deck will work with this system. You can also use regular playing cards — think Spades/Swords, Clubs/Wands, Hearts/Cups, Diamonds/Pentacles (you just won't have the Major Arcana or the Pages in the Court). I even used an Uno deck once, taking out the Zeros, Skips, Reverses, and other word cards. It was a little bit metaphysical emergency and a whole lot of just wanting to see if it could be done. It can.

Okay — so, in the Celtic Cross, you have ten basic positions which we talk about below. Some readers also use an eleventh card called a Significator ("S" in the diagram). The Significator card represents you or the situation about which you're doing the reading and helps you focus on the question. The way you pick this card is to decide which one you're using, go through the deck and pull it out before shuffling. I generally don't use a Significator because whichever card you choose is taken out of the equation, so to speak, and I like to have all cards at my disposal for the message to come through loud and clear.

The Celtic Cross

Now, about this Celtic Cross—here's what it looks like all laid out:

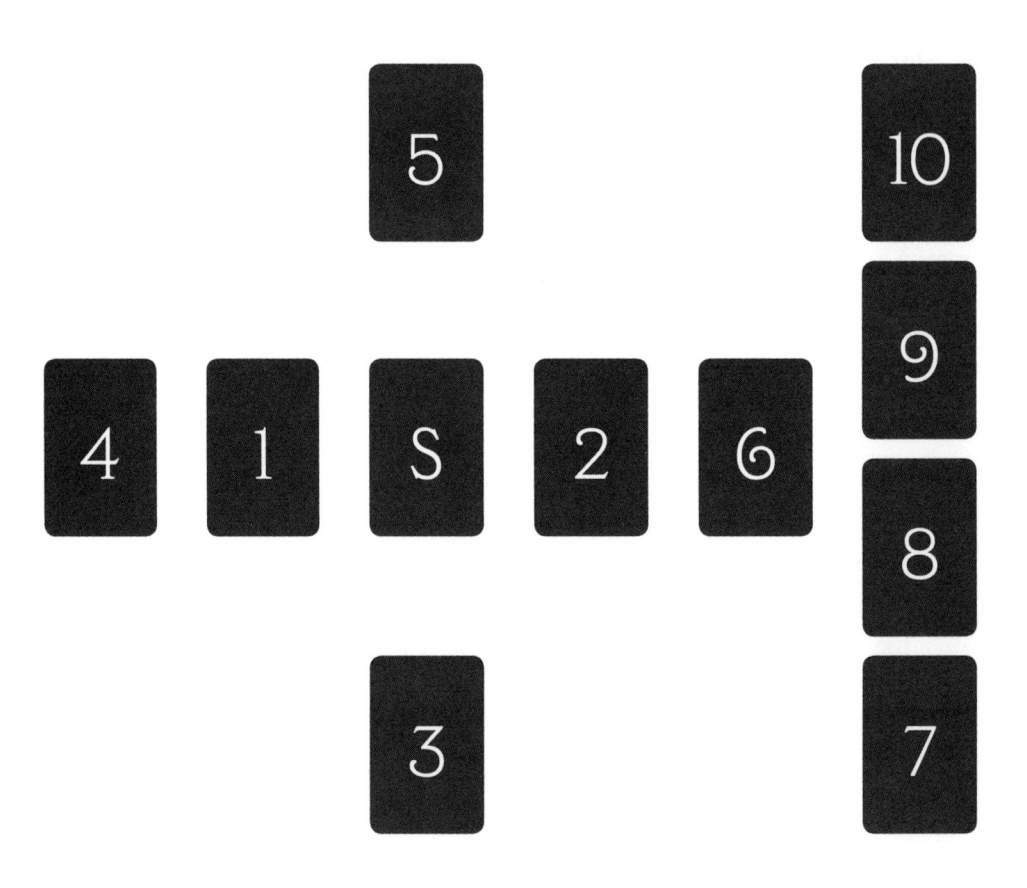

Position S—The Significator

This is the card you select from the deck to represent you or the situation (optional)

Position 1—The Situation

This is what's going on now, what the question is about.

Position 2—The Crossing

Affects the situation positively or negatively.

Position 3—The Base

What the question is REALLY about. Sometimes completely unrelated to Position 1—but that's a whole other book.

Position 4—The Past

Doesn't matter. It's behind you and you can't change it. If you'd like to know how you managed to land yourself in your current pickle, then by all means read it. I generally don't—first rule of Scot driving: what is behind you doesn't matter.

Position 5—The Crown

This position shows the best possible outcome if everything stays exactly as it is right now.

Position 6—The Future

What could come to pass in the near future. **Note:** near future is usually within two weeks, more or less. Use a pencil to mark your calendar, just in case.

Position 7—The Self

This is you and how you feel about what's going on—how it affects you physically, emotionally, spiritually, ergonomically, etc.

Position 8—Outside Influences

No, not trees and oceans and Nature. The Environment card shows the people and circumstances around you, the support group you've constructed.

Position 9—Hopes and Fears

Pretty easy—what you're afraid will happen or what you hope will happen.

Position 10—The Outcome

What could happen as a result of everything else; the Outcome is never, EVER carved in stone—it can be changed if you want it badly enough.

The Three-Card Reading

The Three-Card Reading is even easier—three cards laid out side by side. Of course, upright and reversed meanings still apply:

Position 1—The Past

In the book, read this as card #4 in the Celtic Cross, The Past.

Position 2—The Present

Read this as card #1 in the Celtic Cross, The Situation Card.

Position 3—The Future

Read this as card #10 in the Celtic Cross, The Outcome.

The One-Card Reading

Lastly, we have the One-Card Reading. Use the positional meanings for card #10, The Outcome. You ask the question, draw a card, look it up. Can't get any simpler than that.

Again—and I can't stress it enough—what the Tarot shows is only a snapshot, a captured moment in time reflecting a possible outcome. Results may vary, some restrictions apply, void where prohibited. Outcomes can and do change, depending on what steps we take between the reading and what happens as a result of those steps.

With that being said, now it's your turn. Pick up the cards and get busy.

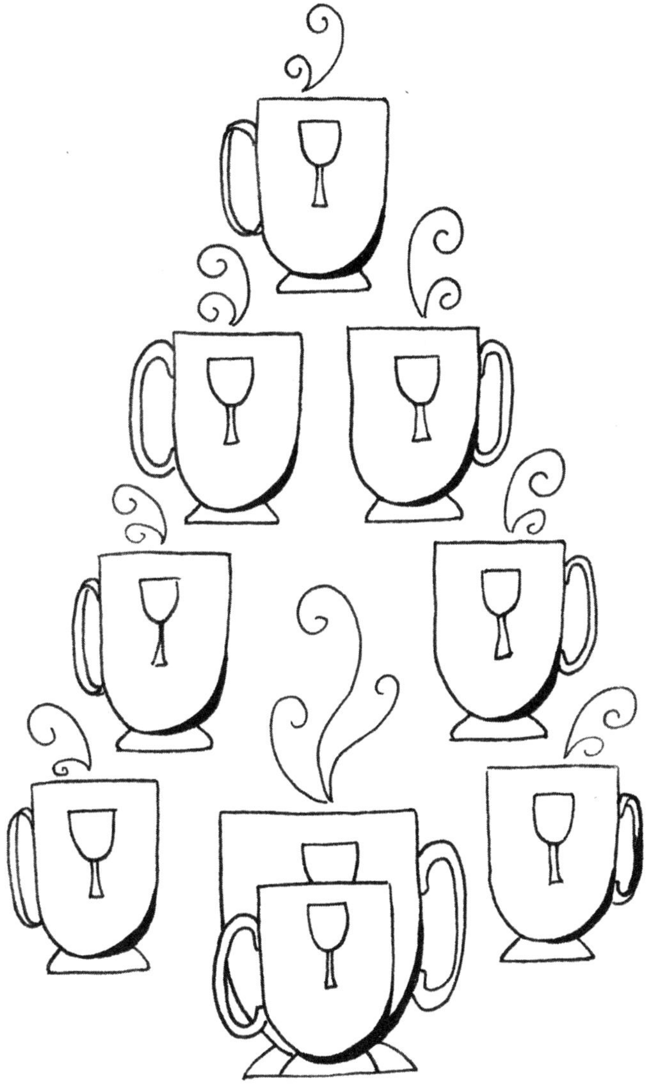

"The cards give you images and symbols to focus your vague intentions and transform them into action. Your will is the magic. In other words, you are the magic. If you can create something in your heart and then act on it to make it happen, that is magic. Very simple, very straightforward—no witches, no spells, and no broomsticks."

—Theresa Francis-Cheung
Teen Tarot: What the Cards Reveal About You and Your Future

The Tarot Cards

The Majors

0. The Fool

The Fool is just starting out on his grand adventure and not quite watching where he is going. He may have a plan, he may not—who cares? This is a card of innocence and bright-eyed optimism, but not necessarily caution or prudence. He denotes a beginning of some sort. It may indicate travel, or at the very least a change of view.

Meaning In a Nutshell:
Beginnings

Position 1—The Situation

Upright:
Think of it as your own personal "magical mystery tour" into the great unknown. You are starting out on a new path. The adventure is just beginning and the day is bright and promising.

Reversed:
You are contemplating what may turn out to be a very wrong move and loud warning bells are sounding the alarm. Fear of the unknown may be the reason you are not moving forward.

Position 2
—The Crossing

Upright:
Your enthusiasm and spontaneity are your biggest assets and the time has come for you to shine. Trust your instincts and take a great big leap of faith, knowing that the pieces will fall into place.

Reversed:
Your lack of experience is adversely affecting the situation and a lack of preparation isn't helping any either. It's time to admit that there is a whole lot of energy is being wasted.

Position 3—The Base

Upright:
Never fear. You will learn what you need to know as you go forward. Your future is so bright you may need to dig those old Ray-Bans out.

Reversed:
You have gotten in way over your head. Obsessive behavior may have been a factor, but having a closed mind about potential solutions isn't going to help anyone.

Position 4—The Past

Upright:
You've already made your break for freedom. Try to remember why you did it and recapture the initial enthusiasm that set you on this new road to begin with.

Reversed:
Your past mistakes are coming back to haunt you and a continued failure to tie up all the loose ends are wreaking havoc. Naiveté and gullibility play a major role.

Position —The Crowning

Upright:
You need a fresh outlook and a new attitude in order to resolve the current drama. Expect the unexpected and be ready to roll with the upcoming changes as they occur.

Reversed:
If you have to stop and ask yourself whether or not it's a good idea, it's not. Don't go against your gut instincts for a fleeting bit of fun and frivolity.

Position 6—The Future

Upright:
The chance or opportunity you have been waiting for might be just around the corner and the time to prepare for it is before it arrives. Have a suitcase ready just in case.

Reversed:
Picture yourself standing at a crossroads. One direction is clearly marked "Right Way," the other "Wrong Way." Think carefully before making any decisions.

Position 7—The Self

Upright:
Doing your best to remain positive, optimistic, and energetic is great, but these qualities alone will not help you much unless you take action to move forward. Put that energy to use!

Reversed:
The rose-colored glasses can only mask so much. You need to acknowledge that a lack of focus has landed you in this position. Distraction has become a major problem and...look, a monkey...

Position 8 —Outside Influences

Upright:
The people around you who love and care about you are supportive and enthusiastic about your successes. Take advantage of your built-in cheering squad and ask them for their advice and guidance.

Reversed:
To say you are not feeling the love is an understatement. If this change is something you feel strongly about, you may have to go it alone without your network backing you up.

Position 9
—Hopes and Fears

Upright:
You are longing for a change, of scenery or just about anything else different that it is right now. Ready for a fresh, new start and beginning, you feel ready to take the risk.

Reversed:
You are unable to concentrate and focus on your goal, taking too many side tangents and fretting about things that will matter not a whit in the long run.

Position 10
—The Outcome

Upright:
Everything's done. All that's left now is to wave goodbye at the old road you were on before turning to face the bright, new future in front of you.

Reversed:
In spite of all the red flags, you are still in danger of heading down the highway to heck. There's still time to change the road you're on, so heed the warnings.

1. The Magician

The Magician is a take-charge kind of guy, able to manipulate the surroundings to manifest his desires. He possesses knowledge and mastery of the elements and strives to take the higher road, but is not always above using them for his own personal gain. He brings the message that the power is in your own hands—use it wisely.

Meaning In a Nutshell:
Empowerment

Position 1—The Situation

Upright:
Yes, as a matter of fact, you ARE all that and a bag of chips! You are in complete control and have the power to manifest what you want to your little heart's content.

Reversed:
Your behavior isn't constructive; it's destructive and it is causing difficulty and delays. You're taking the phrase "my way or the highway" a bit too literally. It's not all about you.

Position 2

—The Crossing

Upright:
You have the capacity to take the reins and take charge of the situation, but you are going to have to take the initiative to do it through self-determination and concentration.

Reversed:
Your expectations aren't exactly realistic right now; if you're not careful and alert, someone will be at your side trying to sell you something you really don't want to buy.

Position 3—The Base

Upright:
You may be skilled in both words and works, but your creativity and ingenuity is where you will truly shine. There must be balance. Remember, as above, so below.

Reversed:
Your mouth might be writing a check you won't be able to pay when it comes time to settle up. Overconfidence is a concern when the ability doesn't match the ego.

Position 4—The Past

Upright:
You have gotten a reputation for being a "go-to" kind of person, able to work miracles and produce new growth from even the most barren wasteland.

Reversed:
Your expectations greatly exceeded your accomplishments. Quit resting on your laurels and get busy. Nobody wants to hear about how great you did it back in the day.

Position —The Crowning

Upright:
It is time to take charge of the situation and utilize the power that is within your grasp. Success is assured if you but let others see the real you: calm, confident and competent.

Reversed:
Twice the pride, double the fall. Arrogance will be your undoing if you can't deliver on your promises. Ask for help before you get in too deeply to recover quickly or at least discreetly.

Position 6—The Future

Upright:
There will be an opportunity that presents itself and you will be the only person capable of pulling the tablecloth from under the dishes without breaking nary a one.

Reversed:
Beware of something that sounds too good to be true as it usually is and you won't find out until it's too late. Do your homework *before* you agree.

Position 7—The Self

Upright:
No matter what modest face you may show to those who seek your special skills, you have nothing but the utmost of confidence. Don't get swept away by the compliments, even if they are true.

Reversed:
It may not be immediately apparent, but you are not the one pulling the strings. Someone is pulling yours instead, but only if you're too weak-willed or indecisive to allow it.

Position 8 —Outside Influences

Upright:
You are blessed with an environment conducive honing your new skills. These are the people who will smile indulgently as you blow something up while experimenting. Just don't abuse their good nature.

Reversed:
Everyone and everything appears to have no function except to throw hindrances, difficulties, and delays in your path. There isn't anywhere you are going to find a sympathetic ear, short of getting a cat.

Position 9
—Hopes and Fears

Upright:
Secretly you may be harboring a desire to be the one everyone looks up to as an authority. For that matter, it might not even be a secret; you want to be calling the shots, period.

Reversed:
You are deathly afraid of being found out to be a complete fraud, exposed and hung out to dry by all those who you think have doubted your abilities all along.

Position 10
—The Outcome

Upright:
Show the world that you have the will and courage to succeed and, most of all, that you are humble. Nobody loves a show-off, but it's not bragging if you can really pull it off!

Reversed:
This isn't going to be a good trip; best to get out at the next stop and wait for another bus. The foundation you built upon is shaky at best, risky at worst.

2. The High Priestess

Lady of Mystery, Queen of the Moon, Mistress of Magick—these are but a few of the titles for The High Priestess. The Keeper of Secrets won't give you the answers you seek, no matter how hard you beg, whine, or plead. Instead, she will teach you to listen to your own inner voice and challenge you to reach deep inside to find your own answers.

Meaning in a Nutshell:
Intuition

Position 1—The Situation

Upright:
You've got that knowing smile like a Cheshire cat and you're not sharing any of your secrets. Listen to the little voice inside, the one that has all the answers, and keep your own counsel.

Reversed:
Oh, someone has done it now—the cat's out of the bag and there's no putting her back. Something that should have stayed hidden is out in plain sight and its effects will be far reaching.

Position 2 —The Crossing

Upright:
You need more information before you can make an informed decision, and there is one close to you who may have the answers you seek.

Reversed:
Warning: subterfuge is alive, well, and living near you. Information is being deliberately withheld from you for the gain of others, so don't believe everything you hear.

Position 3—The Base

Upright:
Water is the element of intuition and emotion, so feel it flowing through you, bringing enlightenment and awakening your subconscious. In other words, be mysterious and trust your instincts—they're spot on.

Reversed:
Be careful who you trust, because there are those of weak and shallow character who would love to see you fail. Don't establish your self-worth by the yardstick of those who don't appreciate you.

Position 4—The Past

Upright:
You have learned much by keeping your mouth closed and your eyes and ears open. Don't dwell on the past; just tuck it away for further use down the road.

Reversed:
The roots of the situation were planted in shallow and conceited soil, and have produced nothing but bitter fruit. Don't place the blame on others without accepting your fair share.

Position —The Crowning

Upright:
Resist the urge to run to tell everyone you know what you know. Don't be afraid of your untapped potential. Nurture it; allow yourself to grow and expand.

Reversed:
Loose lips sink ships and yours is taking on water. Stop now before you say something you may regret in the future. Some things are simply better left unsaid.

Position 6—The Future

Upright:
You have a guiding force coming to you in the form of a teacher or mentor. Keep your eyes open, as you never know what form he/she will take or what lesson they have to teach you.

Reversed:
Beware of the blind leading the blind and don't place your trust easily. Your light will attract psychic vampires (yes, they are real) like crazy if you're not careful.

Position 7—The Self

Upright:
Listen to your inner voice and act upon its advice without stopping to second guess. You already have the answer you want; why get a second opinion?

Reversed:
No one is going to be fooled by the airs you put on if your actions say otherwise. It is easy to spot a shallow person, especially if they're pretending not to be.

Position 8 —Outside Influences

Upright:
Things may seem like a topsy turvey Wonderland, but to you it just seems natural. The mystical and magical have taken root and opened you up to the possibilities before you.

Reversed:
Not everyone who acts friendly is a friend and not everyone who acts as an enemy is one. The lines between good and bad are so muddled, keep your eyes open and your mouth closed.

Position 9

—Hopes and Fears

Upright:
You are inspired to tap into your creative potential and create the spiritual reality you want, but no one is going to give you that gift unless you take it for yourself.

Reversed:
You are wasting your talents on fluff and frippery. Preoccupation with things useless in the long run is a big waste of time, energy, and effort.

Position 10

—The Outcome

Upright:
Just like the *Mona Lisa*, your smile is enigmatic, because you know that all the answers you seek have been inside you all along. Don't second guess yourself and quit over-thinking the situation.

Reversed:
The advice you are getting is wrong, wrong, wrong, and you should resist the urge to fill in the gaps with assumptions and suppositions. Superficiality doesn't become you.

3. The Empress

Affectionately known as the "booty card," the earthy and sensual Empress appears in situations involving sex and/or fertility, and represents motherhood in its many forms. A creative sort who really digs her creature comforts, she would have been right at home at Woodstock, dancing and celebrating life, making sure everyone was feeling the love (and getting enough to eat).

Meaning in a Nutshell:
Fertility

Position 1—The Situation

Upright:
If it is the pitter-patter of little feet that you are longing for, this is the lady you want to see. She smiles on your endeavors, giving you the encouragement you need to succeed.

Reversed:
When Momma ain't happy, ain't nobody happy. The situation you're in is a no-go, completely nonproductive. It could be that attitudes are in immediate need of adjustment.

Position 2 —The Crossing

Upright:
There may be an impending birth, but that doesn't have to mean it is a child. It could be a great new idea or concept that is still in the incubation stage.

Reversed:
There could be problems with promiscuity or infidelity. Indiscretions or false promises made in the heat of the moment are casting a shadow on the current situation.

Position 3—The Base

Upright:
Getting your needs met is paramount, but fortunately this isn't going to be difficult. You'll connect in a big way to Mr./Miss Right or Right Now, at least on a physical level.

Reversed:
Someone is not being entirely truthful in matters of the bedroom, perhaps saying they are a lot more satisfied than they truly are. Trust your intuition and tell your hormones to chill out.

Position 4—The Past

Upright:
You had a strong maternal influence in your life. It may not have been your actual mom, but someone has taught you how to be gentle and encouraging rather than harsh and critical.

Reversed:
You may have a mother complex, such as being domineered by an overbearing one, ignored by an apathetic one, or feeling the emptiness of not having one at all.

Position —The Crowning

Upright:
The creative juices are flowing and now is the time to act upon them. Use your passion wisely and productively, knowing your hard work will be recognized and pay off.

Reversed:
The seeds of your idea are falling on barren soil and will not bear fruit. The timing isn't right or it needs tweaking before it will do anything other than wither on the vine.

Position 6—The Future

Upright:
If you are in a relationship (or would like to be), there promises to be a fun- and delight-filled evening, or even a whole weekend. Don't hold back; let your passions run wild.

Reversed:
On the relationship front, dissatisfaction makes life uncomfortable or downright unbearable. Don't stoop to game playing or let yourself be manipulated, either sexually or emotionally.

Position 7—The Self

Upright:
You give of yourself freely and without reservation. But beware: there are many who would abuse your good nature. Choose wisely and save your favors only for those deserving of them.

Reversed:
Vanity does not suit you. Don't be materialistic, defining those around you by how much they make, what they look like, how they dress, or what kind of car they drive.

Position 8 —Outside Influences

Upright:
You are surrounded by an environment that is as relaxed and comfortable. Now would be a good time to rest up so that you can start planning for the next step.

Reversed:
You feel about as welcome as an ant at a picnic and just about as significant. This is a depressing environment and not one where you'll get a lot accomplished.

Position 9 —Hopes and Fears

Upright:

Your wish list contains abundance, fulfillment, good luck, and fertility, allowing for new growth as well as nurturing the existing.

Reversed:

Your authority is being disrespected all the way around, and to make matters worse, on the male front, there could be an issue with impotence. Relax. Breathe. Repeat.

Position 10—The Outcome

Upright:

If yours was a yes/no question: the answer is a resounding *yes*. Get ready for the good life, because it is getting ready for you. Wishes can come true.

Reversed:

The door just slammed shut on your question and discussions are closed. Either the timing is wrong or the whole situation is off; but either way, it ain't gonna happen.

4. The Emperor

Whether you call him Father, The Man, or The Boss, The Emperor is where the buck stops, period. He rules with a firm hand and has no problem detaching himself enough from the situation to be judge, jury, and if need be, executioner. A graduate of the school of hard knocks, he is still willing to listen as you try to explain your latest fiasco.

Meaning in a Nutshell:
Authority

Position 1—The Situation

Upright:
Order, rules, and structure play a major role. The hierarchy of things is of the ultimate importance and heaven forbid someone attempts to upset the apple cart.

Reversed:
You are chafing under the constraints of dominance. Someone else is running the show and not to your liking. You may feel that you are being bullied or are the object of prejudice.

Position 2 —The Crossing

Upright:
The need for cooler heads and logical thinking prevails. There may be a need for someone to step up and assume leadership to right the helm of a listing ship—you, perhaps?

Reversed:
Impatience could cause you to slip up and miss important details that will come back to haunt you later on. Beware of the flashy displays; they could be overcompensating for a lack of substance.

Position 3—The Base

Upright:
Your ambitions are healthy, balanced, and within the reach of your abilities. Use the wisdom of your experience to guide you. Learn from your mistakes, as well as the mistakes of others.

Reversed:
The decisions you are making are neither well thought out or wise in any way, and the ultimate result will be the loss of your dignity if you are not careful.

Position 4—The Past

Upright:
You have had a very strong positive paternal influence in your life. It may not have been your actual Dad, but someone has taught you how to be authoritative and a good leader, rather than a tyrant.

Reversed:
You may have a father complex, such as being domineered by an overbearing one, ignored by an apathetic one, or feeling the emptiness of not having one at all.

Position —The Crowning

Upright:
Your ambitions will become your successes if you continue to work hard and ethically towards your goals. Take care to think before acting, and maintain control, no matter how excited you get.

Reversed:
Success: you're doing it wrong. Epic Fail is where you are headed if you don't change your path. Someone else is pushing your buttons, and they consider you to be expendable.

Position 6—The Future

Upright:
There is a strong influence that will aid you if asked, someone in the position to offer invaluable assistance and information. You're entering into a competitive situation, so keep a level head.

Reversed:
Egos run amok, so don't get caught up in the "better than you" game. Playing the dozens might seem fun at first, but in truth, it is hurtful and serves no purpose.

Position 7—The Self

Upright:
You are a natural-born leader, and everyone looks to you for advice and guidance. Your quiet authority speaks volumes without saying a word, your very presence commanding attention.

Reversed:
It's time to pull up those big kid underpants—you are acting in a childish manner, refusing to take responsibility for yourself. In fact, you're not being taken seriously at all.

Position 8 —Outside Influences

Upright:
You exist and even thrive on order and structure, and it is critical for you to have things in their proper place. You have your own unique—sometimes obsessive—way of doing stuff.

Reversed:
Just because you got called down for talking in the library is no cause to burn it down. Rebellion for no reason is just wasted energy that could be better spent elsewhere.

Position 9

—Hopes and Fears

Upright:
Your secret desire is to have the power that authority brings and hope that you will finally get the respect you feel you deserve. Remember, you only get what you are willing to work for.

Reversed:
There is a strong fear of losing control, and losing grip on the current situation. What you don't understand is that your grasp is tenuous at best and imaginary at worst.

Position 10

—The Outcome

Upright:
You have fought hard to get where you are. Now is the time to acknowledge your successes, make note of and learn from your past mistakes, and starting planning your next conquest.

Reversed:
Your ego is completely out of hand. Wielding your authority like a sword won't win you any friends, but it will win you the reputation of being a petty tyrant and a bully.

5. The Hierophant

The High Priest or Hierophant doesn't have to be a member of the clergy. He can be a respected teacher or counselor, or someone you hold in high regard. There could be an impending marriage or it could be a gentle nudge towards taking up a more spiritual path, such as joining an order or other organization of religion.

Meaning in a Nutshell:
Traditional

Position 1—The Situation

Upright:
You are comfortable within the familiar constraints of the current situation, and enjoying the routine. Conformity, order, playing well with others, and coloring within the lines are of the utmost importance.

Reversed:
This can indicate a zealot, someone who believes what they believe to an extreme or fanatical degree and will go to any lengths to convert others to their way of thinking.

Position 2 —The Crossing

Upright:
Here's a call for order and the boundaries that the familiar brings. Which serves you better — to conform and leave things as they are or branch out into great unknown?

Reversed:
Your behavior is off the chain and needs reining in. It is okay to think outside the box, but at least keep the box in sight as you unleash your creative genius.

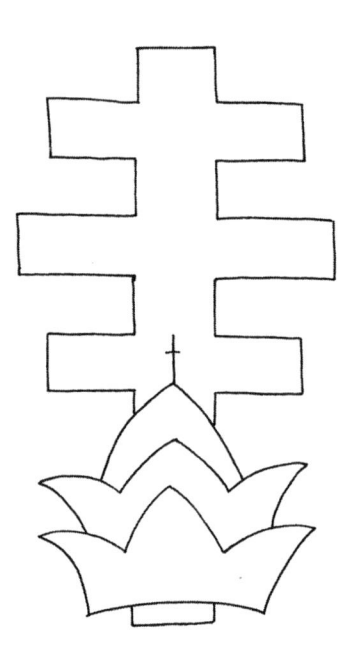

Position 3—The Base

Upright:
This might be a situation involving spiritual commitment of some sort, and there could be questions involving both your morals and your integrity. Choose your alliances wisely and carefully.

Reversed:
You're being impossible and inflexible, refusing to give quarter when you know full well you may be in the wrong. Lighten up and get over yourself. Just. Chill.

Position 4—The Past

Upright:
Yours is a background rich in tradition—conservative, practical, and very structured. You may have for a time thrived in this atmosphere, but kept looking out the window for something more.

Reversed:
What you believed to be true may have been based on appearances and caused a great deal of disillusionment when you found out the truth. Opening your eyes isn't always a painless process.

Position —The Crowning

Upright:
Pause to take stock in your interests. Is there something you've always wanted to pursue? The teacher you need may make an appearance to help you decide on the next step.

Reversed:
You are more concerned with how things appear than how they truly are—it should be the other way around. Build your foundation on solid ground so that your effort won't be wasted.

Position 6—The Future

Upright:
Someone could be getting ready to enter into a formal agreement, such as marriage or other spiritual contracts. There is a need for advice and guidance, so if it's you, be sure to get it.

Reversed:
Your non-traditional way of thinking may be a breath of fresh air into the predictable stuffiness, but make sure you are up-front about your reasons for being different.

Position 7—The Self

Upright:
You can be counted on to keep a level head and cool demeanor no matter how hot it gets in the kitchen, which will work to your benefit in the long run.

Reversed:
Don't even try to pretend that you don't see the elephant in the living room. Ignoring the problems simply will not make them go away.

Position 8 —Outside Influences

Upright:
You may be finding that the day-to-day grind has become humdrum. Try varying your daily routine just to shake things up a bit.

Reversed:
There is information that is being withheld from you by the powers that be, and you are on a strictly need-to-know basis. Right now, it appears, you do not need to know.

Position 9
—Hopes and Fears

Upright:
You want a commitment from someone else, a suitor perhaps, or you may be longing to share your knowledge with others as a teacher. Look to yourself for the validation you need.

Reversed:
Is that a little over the top? I can never tell, but others can. Let the dust from your recent eccentricity settle and make its way into yesterday's news.

Position 10
—The Outcome

Upright:
A marriage or other form of alliance is in the works, and a great bond of trust will be established. The union will be a blessed one, shower gifts all around.

Reversed:
The truth is so distorted, even the mouths twisting the facts around are starting to believe it as gospel. Question the authority if you don't understand, and challenge it if you don't agree.

6. The Lovers

In the beginning, The Lovers card depicted a man trying to choose between two very different women: one virtuous young lady in white and the other wantonly clad in the devil's red, clearly intent on corrupting the morals of the confused young man. There are valid and compelling arguments to be made for both sides.

**Meaning in a Nutshell:
Choices**

Position 1—The Situation

Upright:
There is a decision to be made and no getting around it. It could be in either your personal or professional life, and the chances you are already aware of it and just putting it off are excellent.

Reversed:
Someone (hopefully not you) is infuriating everyone around them by their refusal to grow up and commit themselves to one course of action rather than scattering their energies to the wind.

Position 2 —The Crossing

Upright:
Start making plans for the immediate future as there may be an opportunity for short-term travel. Either way, there's still that pesky decision hanging out there, waiting for you to make it.

Reversed:
Infidelity is in the air: someone who has professed strong feelings in the past may not be feeling the same now. Be honest with yourself and what you want.

Position 3—The Base

Upright:
The time may be approaching to take your growing relationship to the next stage by upping the commitment level. Talk it over with the other party or parties involved.

Reversed:
Hurt feelings, turbulent emotions, high drama— someone's inability to "step up to the plate" in a relationship has caused quite a rift, in spite of all the viable arguments presented to them.

Position 4—The Past

Upright:
Your high moral fiber and scruples have helped you to make good, solid decisions in the past. You have strong personal values, and a high level of integrity.

Reversed:
You're never one to say no to a particularly enticing temptation, especially if you think you won't get caught. Yours has been a checkered past, fraught with bad choices.

Position —The Crowning

Upright:
A personal relationship may be ready to move to the next level, requiring a decision on your part to get it there. Don't allow yourself to be talked into anything you are not ready for.

Reversed:
There could be interference as in "it just happened; he/she didn't really mean anything to me." If you hear those words, the third party is hearing them too in an effort to pacify you both.

Position 6—The Future

Upright:
Your relationship is growing and the ties that bind so lovingly are getting deeper. If it is just a casual thing, you'll find you want more and more.

Reversed:
There are ties, all right, but they're not the deep and lasting kind. This is a more of a "just for right now" kind of relationship (with emphasis on the "right now").

Position 7—The Self

Upright:
You take the higher ground and do the right thing because it is the right thing to do, not because you have to or because someone else is watching.

Reversed:
Sincerity is something that you'll find harder and harder to fake. You can't play a player, so cut your losses and 'fess up if you haven't been up-front and forthright about your feelings.

Position 8 —Outside Influences

Upright:
You have a harmonious staging area where you are able to work through your "what if" situations. Go there and make your plans, organize your thoughts, and sort out your priorities.

Reversed:
Beware of the wolf in sheep's clothing. Not to be trusted, he/she won't care if your reputation lies shattered on the rocks. In plainer speak, the emotion is lust, not love.

Position 9
—Hopes and Fears

Upright:
Your emotions run strong and deep and may be all-consuming in their frequency. If you haven't professed your feelings do so, even if only to put yourself out of your misery.

Reversed:
Envy isn't considered the sixth deadly sin for nothing, and wanting to see the downfall of others for your pleasure will bring you to no good end.

Position 10
—The Outcome

Upright:
If you are looking to get married or engaged, or form another type of partnership, it's looking good. Once you have made your choice, commit fully in order to succeed.

Reversed:
If you are longing for a loving and lasting partnership, this isn't it. This is a temporary arrangement only, based on shallow feelings, surface appearances, and physical urges only.

7. The Chariot

Crack that whip and give the past the slip! You're on a mission and have the drive and determination to face up to any challenges along your path. You've got the reins to drive as far and fast as you like. With a strong hand and a steady nerve, you can guide this ride to wherever your dreams take you.

Meaning in a Nutshell: Progress

Position 1—The Situation

Upright:
Your pioneering spirit is pushing you forward. If you haven't set your goals yet, stop putting it off and decide where you are going already. There could be a message coming your way.

Reversed:
Your ambition isn't healthy or productive. Your goals are too generalized to meet, let alone succeed. Focus on what you want out of life and decide exactly what path you will take to get there.

Position 2—The Crossing

Upright:
You have your eyes on the prize and nothing is making you look away. Stick to the game plan, and rely on your strong self discipline to keep you straight.

Reversed:
Unless you can get your ship righted, it is going to sink. Don't let your arrogance and pride get in the way of learning the lessons needed to progress.

Position 3—The Base

Upright:
Yours is truly a warrior spirit and your self control is admirable. Reassess your plans often to see if there are any areas or details that require tweaking or adjusting.

Reversed:
You are having some major inner conflicts and you are about to lose your way. As the old saying goes, he who chases two rabbits catches neither.

Position 4—The Past

Upright:
Careful planning and decisive action when the time was right has brought you to where you are now. You have been self-disciplined both mentally and emotionally.

Reversed:
The expectations and standards that you hold for others are unreasonably high to be realistic. Your ideas are old and outdated—it's time for an extreme outlook makeover.

Position —The Crowning

Upright:
Your victory and triumph over adversity is imminent, provided you stay the course and don't waver in your resolve. Don't get overconfident, though—you'll lose your competitive edge.

Reversed:
Too many loose ends left hanging has made failure inescapable. Drowning your sorrows might seem like a good idea, but substance abuse will take you even further away from your target.

Position 6—The Future

Upright:
There's an opportunity en route, so be ready to reach out and grab that ring as it flies by. Resist the urge to flaunt your brilliance to those around you.

Reversed:
Your pride is in danger of making you miss a golden opportunity. Don't be so rigid and inflexible that you can't amend your plans if you need to.

Position 7—The Self

Upright:
You are (or could be) one of the most focused people you know, grounded and centered in the pursuit of what you want out of life. No waffling back and forth for you.

Reversed:
Don't be tempted by nefarious schemes to cut corners. Cheaters never win in the long run (read: Karma) and if exposed, your reputation would take a blow it won't recover from.

Position 8 —Outside Influences

Upright:
Yours is a very high energy environment—those around you are amped up and focused on the task at hand. Be open to new ideas from unusual sources.

Reversed:
It's official: the inmates are running the asylum. Chaos reigns supreme and no one knows what anyone else is doing. Don't make any decisions until things quiet down.

The Chariot

Position 9

—Hopes and Fears

Upright:
You're the mail room clerk who dreams of impressing the boss with a fabulous new idea, allowing you to move past the naysayers and straight into the corner office with the view.

Reversed:
You've taken a strange turn down "It's All About Me" Road, just a little ways away from "I'm In Charge and Don't You Forget It" Boulevard. Get a grip.

Position 10

—The Outcome

Upright:
The power is yours, and you wield it with a strong and sure hand. If you keep your cool and don't lose your competitive edge, your victory is assured.

Reversed:
Without a major change in priorities, you are doomed to fail. Re-examine what it is you think you want to see if it is something you really need.

8. Strength

Forget lifting weights. Inner strength is the kind that enables you to walk away from a situation you know is detrimental or take on a challenge that terrifies you. It can be as complex as defending a child from an abuser at the risk of your own life or as simple as resisting that second piece of pie.

**Meaning in a Nutshell:
um…Strength**

Position 1—The Situation

Upright:
Your radiance acts as a magnet for those who find these qualities lacking in themselves. No one has to steal your energy; you give it freely to all you encounter.

Reversed:
You are feeling vulnerable, victimized, and as weak as you could possibly be. Get past the "poor me" nonsense—a defeatist attitude will help no one, least of all yourself.

Position 2

—The Crossing

Upright:
You have the power to harness the destructive forces, provided that you remember the old saying that you catch more flies with honey than with vinegar.

Reversed:
Whatever is going on, you are making it worse by overdramatizing the issues. The tighter you hold, the looser your grasp and that which you value will slip through your fingers.

Position 3—The Base

Upright:
No knee jerk reactions please, just harmonious balance and thoughtful decision-making skills necessary. Get and maintain your composure; let your charm and charisma take you where you need to be.

Reversed:
Someone's old school control methods are threatening to bring down the whole house. If challenged, they will turn it around on you to divert attention from their own misdeeds. Don't fall in their trap.

Position 4—The Past

Upright:
If someone were to look up empowerment in the dictionary, they'd see your picture. You are the paragon of quiet authority, diplomatic to a fault and admired for your courage and compassion.

Reversed:
Letting others dictate your opinions has led you to where you are now. Your helplessness has drawn in those who would manipulate you, like sharks smelling blood in the water.

Position —The Crowning

Upright:
Muscling your way in isn't the way to go. Gentleness will take you further than you can even dream of. Stay the course, and above all, don't lose your cool.

Reversed:
There's a bull in the china shop and all hell is breaking loose. You're trying too hard to maintain control at the expense of your own reputation.

Position 6—The Future

Upright:
You will have an opportunity to show off your generous nature. Make sure to give for the sake of giving and not for the attention the giving will get you.

Reversed:
There is no need to become argumentative when confronted about your shortcomings; your anger and blustering will only shine an unwanted spotlight on you, faults and all.

Position 7—The Self

Upright:
Know your own self-worth and do not let yourself be taken for granted. You are strong emotionally and blows that would fell a lesser person barely faze you.

Reversed:
If you face your fears head on, you can overcome the obstacles that have been placed before you. If not, nothing changes and you will continue down your destructive path.

Position 8 —Outside Influences

Upright:
You are surrounded by people who allow you the freedom to be yourself. They may rely heavily on your judgment, pulling you in too many directions at once.

Reversed:
There are those who would like nothing better than to see you fail and may even take steps to hasten your descent. You would do well to keep your own counsel.

Position 9

—Hopes and Fears

Upright:
You would like nothing better than to be the hero who sweeps in, ties up all the problems, and tosses them over your shoulder with a well timed, "Oh, it was nothing."

Reversed:
You know that you don't like things as they are, but you feel powerless to change them, knowing all the while that your failure to act will be your downfall in the end.

Position 10

—The Outcome

Upright:
Yours is the violin playing the music that soothes the savage beastie. You are so gentle in your persuasion, most don't even realize they are bending to your will.

Reversed:
That which you crave so desperately is slipping through your fingers, even as you speak. You are trying so desperately to keep control that you are losing it with every step you take.

9. The Hermit

Remember *Star Wars: The Empire Strikes Back*? When Luke takes his journey of self-discovery deep into the swamps of Dagobah, Yoda was his own personal Hermit, urging him on, to get in touch with his inner Jedi, so that he could get on with the business of saving the Universe. Better pack a lunch—it's not always an easy trip.

Meaning in a Nutshell: Introspection

Position 1—The Situation

Upright:
Here's you standing at the foot of the mountain, thinking about the climb ahead. This is going to be a solo trip. Use the alone time to your best advantage.

Reversed:
Don't take your social confinement out on everyone around you—telling everyone over and over how miserable you are will make even your friends leave skid marks getting away.

Position 2 —The Crossing

Upright:
You're having doubts about your current path for good reason—take a little time out to re-examine why you're doing what you're doing. You need to give the matter some deeper thought.

Reversed:
You're not thinking the problem through. If you don't' pause long enough to regroup, you're on a collision course with disaster. Forcing the issue will only make matters worse.

Position 3—The Base

Upright:
You know the difference between right, wrong, and all the shades of gray in between. If it feels right, it likely is. On the other hand, if you have to ask, it's probably not.

Reversed:
You're in over your head—admit it and pull back before it is too late. Nobody wants to hear your excuses; they want to know how you're going to fix the problem.

Position 4—The Past

Upright:
Being in touch with yourself has served you well. You've already done the due diligence and know who you are and where you're going.

Reversed:
Nothing you can do can change anything that has gone before, so it's best to accept it and move forward a little wiser than before.

Position —The Crowning

Upright:
A word of caution to this tale—keep an open mind and you will prevail. Corny but true—flexibility keeps the willow alive, while standing too firm uproots the oak.

Reversed:
There's a fine line between introspect and isolation—don't withdraw so deep inside your own little world that loved ones need a search party to find you.

Position 6—The Future

Upright:
You're going to face a challenge that you're not prepared for. Time to sit this dance out and rethink why you came in the first place.

Reversed:
It's not paranoia if they're really out to get you, but make sure of the threat before you start reinforcing the castle walls. Could be nothing more than idle interest.

Position 7—The Self

Upright:
You see yourself on the path to enlightenment, a solitary soul on life's journey. Whatever the romantic verbiage, you're searching for your own meaning of life.

Reversed:
Lonely—adj. Lonesomeness. Subsequent depression and shunning of social engagements. A generally sucky state of being. Get over it—drag yourself out in public and talk to people already.

Position 8 —Outside Influences

Upright:
Not many fellow travelers at this rest stop—you might feel alone for the moment but you're never alone. Many have walked the road you're on, even if you don't see them.

Reversed:
Just like Greta Garbo, you want to be alone—whether it's due to creative expression or just plain contrariness, you got to get away. Explain this gently but firmly to your loved ones.

The Hermit

Position 9
—Hopes and Fears

Upright:
It won't hurt to go over the plan once more, but trust that you've thought through the problem from every angle. At some point, you have to trust you made the right decision.

Reversed:
Just like visiting NASA doesn't make you an astronaut, acting all dark and mysterious doesn't make you a deep and profound thinker. Don't fool yourself into believing your own hype.

Position 10
—The Outcome

Upright:
Your goal is to live your own personal truth and you're on your way. The care you take to make the right decisions for all concerned will shine through.

Reversed:
Shine your light in those dark corners and expose your flaws, so that they can be put to rights. Time to regroup and rethink the course you've set for yourself.

10. The Wheel of Fortune

Round and round goes The Wheel of Fortune and anybody who says they know where she is going to stop is selling something. Opportunities, both good and bad, disguise themselves in a variety of ways. Preparation is the only way to be ready for whichever way the Wheel chooses to turn, so step up and give her a spin. Feeling lucky?

Meaning in a Nutshell:
Luck

Position 1—The Situation

Upright:
Time to go out on that limb and break out of the comfortable rut you're in. Shake things up a little, and let your mind wander — what's the worst that could happen?

Reversed:
The path you're contemplating is fraught with opportunities — none of them good. Now isn't the time to be taking chances, so sit tight and wait for things to play out.

Position 2 —The Crossing

Upright:
This is something you should seriously consider — it's the vehicle to get you where you're going, although it might be a Yugo instead of the Mercedes you were expecting.

Reversed:
A little bad luck makes you appreciate the good, but it doesn't make the bad any easier to swallow. You're not going to catch a break, so don't make plans expecting it to get better.

Position 3—The Base

Upright:
This is a shining moment for you; things are looking good and all the pieces are falling into place. The brass ring is coming into view — be ready to make a grab for it!

Reversed:
Now is not the time to depend on luck alone — you couldn't catch a break with a butterfly net. Better to count on hard work and elbow grease instead.

Position 4—The Past

Upright:
Getting out of the state you were in has led to great changes. Your decision was the right one at the time and opened many doors for you.

Reversed:
Not even the jaws of life could bust you out of your rut. Your inability to roll with the changes has landed you in your current predicament.

Position —The Crowning

Upright:
Lady Luck is smiling on your current endeavor and you are the golden child. Don't gnaw your nails waiting for the Wheel to turn—enjoy the moment!

Reversed:

Position 6—The Future

Upright:
Don't blink in case you miss it; an opportunity is coming. Get ready to jump up and grab the ring as it passes—luck will be on your side.

Reversed:
Don't even THINK about it. It won't work. The timing isn't right or the planets are out of alignment. Whatever. Don't do it.

Position 7—The Self

Upright:
All the pieces are falling into place for you and everything you touch turns to rainbows and sparkles. It's a good time to be you—appreciate it!

Reversed:
Okay, so your luck isn't the greatest right now. You can't stay on the bottom of the Wheel forever, although it may be taking its time on the way back up.

Position 8 —Outside Influences

Upright:
The environment is right for you to move on up in the world. You've got a supportive network around you—use it considerately for good Karma points.

Reversed:
You're banging your head against the wall. No one is lining up to give you the handout you're looking for. Better stop stalling and handle the problem yourself.

Position 9
—Hopes and Fears

Upright:
All you want is one little break. Just one. Keep the positivity going and don't rely solely on luck — get the hard work out of the way.

Reversed:
You would do well to just accept that not everything is going to go your way all the time. Suck it up and deal with it.

Position 10
—The Outcome

Upright:
The winds of change are blowing your way, so open your sails and let that breezy goodness in. Your destiny is at hand — be prepared for rapid, but good changes.

Reversed:
Sorry, it just ain't happening. Better luck next time. Make notes of what didn't go well, and make a promise to yourself not to do that anymore.

11. Justice

Justice is blind, just desserts, what's good for the goose is good for the gander, etc. — all the clichés apply. This is the "what goes around comes around" card. Legal matters are spotlighted, but at the very least, Karma is leveling the playing field. Whether you have wronged someone or been wronged yourself, it's time to settle up the accounts.

Meaning in a Nutshell: Responsibility

Position 1—The Situation

Upright:
A conflict is coming to the forefront and needs your immediate attention. You are being called to account for your actions or back up your accusations against another.

Reversed:
Whatever nefarious dealings you're up to are coming to light and you may not be off to a good start as far as the judges go — a real "you're in deep excrement" moment.

Position 2 —The Crossing

Upright:
Forewarned is forearmed. Prepare your defense now and expect your argument to be at least heard, if not accepted outright. Lawyer up if you need to.

Reversed:
Now isn't the time to go against the advice of counsel. The odds are stacked against you and the jury already swayed to the opposition. Think before acting.

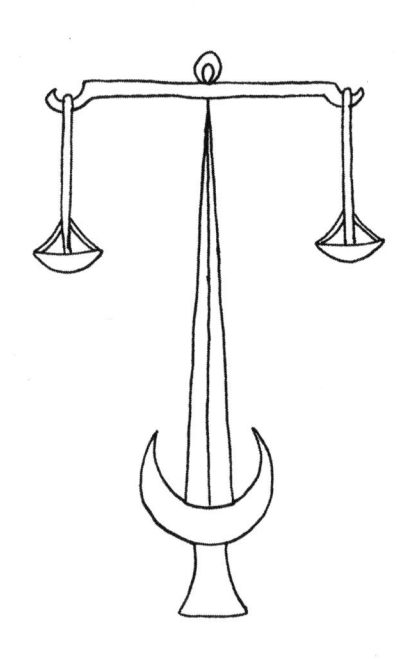

Position 3—The Base

Upright:
Matters are coming to a head. It's time for clearing the air of grievances and petty disagreements. Expect fairness in your dealings and be fair in return.

Reversed:
Intolerance and indecision are dashing your hopes of getting a fair shake. Things definitely aren't going your way, assumptions are made, and incorrect conclusions being drawn.

Position 4—The Past

Upright:
Your integrity in resolving a past issue is showing and those involved know you to be an honorable person. The care you have taken in preserving your reputation shows.

Reversed:
Maybe you weren't always above board in your past dealings, but even if you were, that's not the public opinion. Clear the air, but don't expect everyone to believe it.

Position —The Crowning

Upright:
Standing outside the courtroom, you're next up on the docket. This will be your moment to shine. Prepare your argument and get ready to dazzle the jury—it's a lock.

Reversed:
You're a little downwind of the fan and guess what just hit it. Better start thinking about how you're going to handle the damage control and the subsequent mess.

Position 6—The Future

Upright:
Get ready to gird your loins for battle. The time is coming to take your concerns before a higher authority. Get all your pertinent paperwork in order now.

Reversed:
Brace yourself and don't look for a fair shake—you won't get one. You may need a rowboat and compass to navigate the sea of red tape you'll be facing.

Position 7—The Self

Upright:
Trying to do the right thing is admirable, particularly when it's not what you want to do. Your integrity serves you well and yours is the voice of reason in the madness.

Reversed:
Okay, so you haven't been the most responsible and yeah, the powers that be are going to hold it against you. Try not to draw extra attention to your past transgressions.

Position 8 —Outside Influences

Upright:
You're not alone—you've got more support than you think. When you're on the side of justice and fairness, you can't help but attract those as idealistic as yourself.

Reversed:
You stand accused, but you may or may not be guilty. This may not be the most ideal of circumstances—friends willing to help your case are few and far between.

Position 9
—Hopes and Fears
Upright:
Plain and simple, you want to come out on top in the current conflict. There's nothing like the rush of winning, especially when you know you're in the right.

Reversed:
Fear of loss is a powerful tool—just ask any used car salesman. Don't be so blinded by your desire to win that you lose focus on whether or not you should.

Position 10
—The Outcome
Upright:
All the pieces are falling into place—if it's vindication you're looking for, you've got it. Legal matters will be resolved in your favor and harmony restored. Life is good.

Reversed:
Getting railroaded is never fun. The verdict won't be in your favor and no amount of whining can change it. You may have lost the battle, but maybe not the war.

12. The Hanged Man

Even making no choice is a choice of sorts—The Hanged Man deliberates ad infinitum, often paralyzed into inaction. This isn't always a bad thing. Sometimes you need to step back and take a hard look at what's really going on. There is always a second or third side to the story and it might pay you to investigate further.

**Meaning in a Nutshell:
Decisions**

Position 1—The Situation

Upright:
There's a choice to be made and likely not an easy one. Time to sit this dance out and catch your breath. There's no rush—think about your options.

Reversed:
Chocolate, vanilla…maybe… pistachio? You're holding up the line. Make your choice already and get on with your life. Your indecision is bringing everything good to a grinding halt.

Position 2

—The Crossing

Upright:
Your hands are tied at this point, so use the downtime to your advantage. In the meantime, make yourself useful. Time to dig out the "when I get around to it" list.

Reversed:
If you proceed further based on incorrect information, then you—and you alone—will be the one who others choose to make an example of. Don't accept punishment for another's actions.

Position 3—The Base

Upright:
Offering yourself up as a sacrificial lamb to someone else's cause is noble, but make sure the cause is worthy of your efforts. Do they deserve you?

Reversed:
You are wasting your time—martyrdom is a lonely road to walk and no one is interested in how much you've suffered. Time for a paradigm shift in your personal reality.

Position 4—The Past

Upright:
Self-doubt may be nibbling away at you, but keep in mind that you cannot undo what has already been done. It's best to commit yourself fully and not look back.

Reversed:
You suffered from a lack of structure in your life and learned that not having any rules is a harder life than you would have ever imagined.

Position —The Crowning

Upright:
Trust that your inner voice is giving you the best counsel possible, because it is the one voice that does truly have your best interests at heart.

Reversed:
If you won't take the good advice you're being given, don't ask for it. It's good to have a healthy sense of self, but bad to be obsessed with said self.

Position 6—The Future

Upright:
Time to clear out that emotional closet, get rid of the useless baggage you've been toting around and free yourself. There now. Doesn't that feel better?

Reversed:
You are caught in a prison of your own making, and ignoring the problem won't make it go away. You're so afraid of taking the wrong road that you're not moving forward at all.

Position 7—The Self

Upright:
You're in the "paying your dues" part of the journey. Embrace humility and check your ego at the door. It's time for you to face—and conquer—your fears.

Reversed:
Wallowing in self pity is not a good place to be. Don't take it out on yourself by escaping into substance abuse. You are allowing your energies to be misdirected.

Position 8 —Outside Influences

Upright:
It never hurts to get a second (or third) opinion. You don't necessarily have to follow it, but it will make whoever you ask feel good to be a part of your journey.

Reversed:
Those surround you may feel (even if they don't express it in so many words) that the decision you are contemplating is not for your highest good. It might pay you to listen.

Position 9
—Hopes and Fears

Upright:
Freedom from limitations is a heady thing but it is within your reach if you choose to work for it. Commit yourself and let go of your past preconceptions.

Reversed:
The old adage is true: it is better to remain silent and be thought a fool, than to open your mouth and remove all doubts. Hint: it's time for you to stop talking.

Position 10
—The Outcome

Upright:
Weigh the possibility of gain versus the risks you're considering and don't rush into anything without thinking it through completely. Trust in your ability to make good choices.

Reversed:
Don't make any decisions at this time, especially important life-altering ones. You don't have all the facts and thus cannot form an educated opinion. Quit making excuses for bad behaviors.

13. Death

Don't freak out when you see this card. When Death appears, it almost never means someone is going to die. We all die—it is a vital part of life. It does mean that someone's getting ready to knock over your carefully built house of cards—how well you deal with the aftermath is what defines you as a person.

Meaning in a Nutshell:
Ch-ch-ch—Changes, Baby.

Position 1—The Situation

Upright:
Change is imminent and all up in your face—can't ignore it or go around it. All you can do is try to put a good spin on the upheaval ahead.

Reversed:
Things are about to take a turn for the worse. Better dig out the heavy rain gear, there's a downpour ahead and you're going to get really, really wet.

Position 2 —The Crossing

Upright:
Someone is going to upset your apple cart, but it won't be anything you can't handle. Be flexible; everything is going exactly like it is supposed to.

Reversed:
No one ever said transition is easy—it hurts like hell, even more so when you fight it tooth and nail. Impending changes are for the worse—brace yourself.

Position 3—The Base

Upright:
The unnecessary is being trimmed away in anticipation of new growth ahead. Bless and release those unneeded emotions; they are of no more use to you.

Reversed:
Change is necessary to life. You're prolonging the anxiety. Take a deep breath and yank the band-aid off quickly. Picking around the edges just makes the pain last longer.

Position 4—The Past

Upright:
You perceived yourself to be ready to take a chance and step onto the unfamiliar path before you. You were right to embrace the unknown; you're no stranger to upheaval.

Reversed:
There's no problem with revisiting the past. The problem lies in setting up residence there. Don't dwell—no amount of energy will change anything that happened before.

Position —The Crowning

Upright:
Think of yourself as a phoenix rising from the ashes. You'll get through this—you are the rock, the pillar of strength that everyone looks to for assurance.

Reversed:
Going with the flow has turned into a riptide. You're being pulled under and are in immediate danger of drowning. Let go of what you've got a stranglehold on.

Position 6—The Future

Upright:
Births aren't easy, rebirths even more so. You're going to be liberated from your current woes, so it's time to celebrate and sniff back those tears of nostalgia.

Reversed:
Your rage at the status quo is counterproductive. If you want to see the author of your current misery, just look in the mirror. It's not all about you.

Position 7—The Self

Upright:
Let your inner child out—his/her creativity will be needed for the reconstruction ahead. There is a clean slate being offered. Will you wipe the past clean and start over?

Reversed:
Now isn't the time to slip into dark pits of depression and pessimism. Stay to the light if you want to get through these troubling times. Take a walk or something. Breathe.

Position 8 —Outside Influences

Upright:
You approve and support the changes at hand, but you may need for everyone else to get caught up on your agenda. Give them time to adjust to the new you.

Reversed:
Fighting inescapable change along with incessant complaining is a sure fire way to ensure you'll be doing it alone. Voice your opinion then shut up about it.

Death

Position 9
—Hopes and Fears

Upright:
   While you're not calling for an apocalypse, you're definitely hoping to shake things up. Make sure the dragon is really asleep before you go poking and picking at it.

Reversed:
   You feel like you're the one doing all the work while everyone else gets recess. Make sure that's really the case before you get loud and cry foul.

Position 10
—The Outcome

Upright:
   Out with the old, in with the new — a new beginning is made possible only by an ending. Smile and face the new reality with hope for the future.

Reversed:
   Although you may desperately want it, it's not yet time to cut the cord. There are things left unfinished and until those details are hammered out, you are stuck where you are.

14. Temperance

Rein it in, rookie — it's time to slow your pace, read the map, and check your bearings. You ARE making progress, even if it doesn't feel like it. Every journey is marked with a series of adjustments, some little, some big. Take time out from your busy schedule to smell the roses once in a while. So far, so good.

Meaning in a Nutshell:
Balance

Position 1—The Situation

Upright:
In the balancing act of who you were versus who you are, you're hitting all the marks. Relax and enjoy the tranquility. Peace — you're doing it right.

Reversed:
You've stumbled off the beaten track and lost your way. Are you going to continue making a mess of things or will you stop and ask directions before it's too late?

Position 2 —The Crossing

Upright:
You're on the right path and things are progressing nicely. Don't look for things to start going wrong or they will. Try to stay positive, in spite of potential insecurity.

Reversed:
Your impatience with the lack of progress isn't helping matters at all. In fact, it's getting worse. Your judgment would have to improve to be bad.

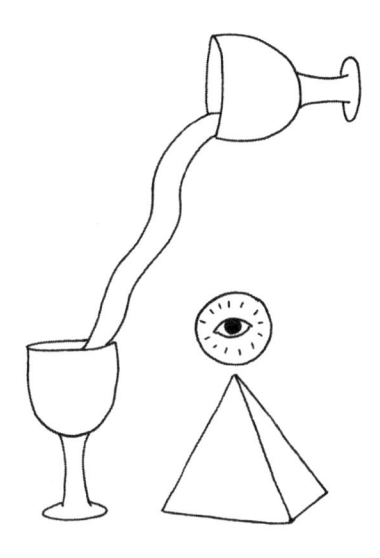

Position 3—The Base

Upright:
Find the center of your internal happy place. Peaceful and harmonious, it is the perfect vacation spot for you to gain confidence and reassurance in your abilities.

Reversed:
Wanting it to be the right choice won't make it so. Your energies are misguided and your unwillingness to compromise in the spirit of fairness will come back to haunt you.

Position 4—The Past

Upright:
The tortoise proved it conclusively: slow and steady wins the race. You've been patient, knowing there are greater rewards to come and they are worth waiting for.

Reversed:
You've placed your trust in those all too willing to take advantage of such an impressionable soul and lost sight of your original purpose.

Position —The Crowning

Upright:
It's all about the balance, Baby. Don't lose sight of the goal but don't forget to have a little fun along the way. Everything in moderation, including chocolate and shoes.

Reversed:
Remember the old adage about the trees, one supple and bending in the wind, the other standing rigid and getting broken by the breeze? Staying flexible = staying sane.

Position 6—The Future

Upright:
You may have a sudden inspirational flash of how to deal with a pesky problem. Now is the time to listen to the voice within and know that it will serve you well.

Reversed:
You must have missed the email about moderation in all things—overindulgence, careless actions, and frivolous spending will get you nothing but deeper and deeper in trouble.

Position 7—The Self

Upright:
You have the willpower and perseverance to succeed in what you set out to do, and you set your own standard for self-worth. Your self-control is admirable.

Reversed:

Position 8 —Outside Influences

Upright:
If other people want to make assumptions and imagine the worst, let them. It's not your place to set things right this time. Just like…um…noses: everyone's got an opinion.

Reversed:
The atmosphere is complete and utter bedlam. You'll be lucky if you can find a quiet spot in which to get in touch with your innermost thoughts.

Position 9
—Hopes and Fears

Upright:
Keep the lines of communication open and you'll receive all the information you need. Drag your keen sense of the obvious out of mothballs—you'll need it.

Reversed:
Your huffing and puffing won't blow the house down. Rest yourself and stop trying to push the river. Soften your approach and let it come to you instead.

Position 10
—The Outcome

Upright:
It is the conviction of your beliefs and the compassion you feel for others, tempered with your senses of right, wrong, and responsibility that will see you through.

Reversed:
Quit chasing your tail and settle back down to business. You can find the right path again, but first you're got to figure out you're on the wrong one.

Temperance

15. The Devil

Too much of a good thing is definitely not a good thing—obsessions are sneaky in the extreme. Whether it's shopping or sex, The Devil get holds and doesn't let go once you're hooked on your drug of choice. "Rock and Roll All Night, Party Every Day" is a great song, but you can't keep that lifestyle up indefinitely without paying the price.

**Meaning in a Nutshell:
Indulgence**

Position 1—The Situation

Upright:
Something has you in thrall. You may be trapped and don't even know it. Take a hard look at what's really important. An immediate sorting out of priorities is in order.

Reversed:
A separation is imminent, either a relationship or situation. It's time to let go and move forward on the road to recovery. Cut your losses while you still can.

Position 2

—The Crossing

Upright:
Temptation isn't always a bad thing, but be sure you understand what you're getting into. Everyone deserves a little fun now and then. Know when to say when.

Reversed:
Beware of false flattery—even if you desperately want to hear those silky words—because it can convince you to go places you don't want to be.

Position 3—The Base

Upright:
Like a fly in a web, you are well and truly caught. Don't be so desperate to have you way at any cost—it may be more expensive than you're willing to pay.

Reversed:
If it looks too good to be true, it probably is. Not paying attention to what's going on around you will mark you as a victim in the making. Stay alert!

Position 4—The Past

Upright:
Making trouble for trouble's sake doesn't do anything except destroy trust. There reaches a point when practical jokes turn mean. Translation: you could have been nicer.

Reversed:
Going along just to hang with the cool kids makes you look like another sheep in the flock. Good thing you figured that out and remembered you have a mind of your own.

Position —The Crowning

Upright:
There are many types of lust, such as for material goods or physical pleasures. Recognize it for what it is and get a grip on your desires. Exercise a little self control.

Reversed:
Although "I'm sorry" never really fixes anything, it's never too late to say it. Remember to forgive yourself your transgressions while you're at it—you need your love too.

Position 6—The Future

Upright:
You are being seriously tempted by forbidden fruit and are afraid of getting your hand smacked if you dare try it. Weigh the advantages—are they worth the risk?

Reversed:
Get ready to take the first step towards a better life. Lighten up a little and release the anger you're carrying. It's time to step into the light again.

Position 7—The Self

Upright:
Look around. The prison you're in should look familiar, you're the one who made it. Therefore, the only person holding you back is you. Now isn't the time for weakness.

Reversed:
Turning over a new leaf can be a scary thing. Get yourself a solid plan on how you're going to make your life better. Make a list, buy some post it notes. Whatever works.

Position 8 —Outside Influences

Upright:
Those around you would happily lead you off to Pleasure Island and laugh when you turn into a donkey just like Pinocchio. Be careful who you associate with.

Reversed:
There are like-minded individuals who will help you get your life back in order if you ask. Get past your pride and admit you need help to conquer your personal demons.

Position 9
—Hopes and Fears

Upright:
Fun, shiny, sparkly—all wonderful things. Have fun chasing them, but leave before the party is over. Last one there is the one who cleans up the mess left behind.

Reversed:
Look for complications to slow you down and try to divert you from your course. Try to see things clearly and objectively— listen to your head, not your heart.

Position 10
—The Outcome

Upright:
When you've lost hope, you've lost everything. Don't be so enamored of material gain that you lose your soul in the process. It won't be worth it in the long run.

Reversed:
Free at last—give those chains a good shake before you cast them off. Then make a note of how they got there, so that you don't get fooled into putting them back on.

16. The Tower

Pride cometh before a fall. The Tower's sole purpose is to shake you up, spin you around, and turn you inside out in the effort to make you come to grips with who you are. When you do lose ground, the higher you are means the farther down you'll tumble. Remember that lightning always strikes the top of the Tower, never the foundation.

Meaning in a Nutshell:
Upheaval

Position 1—The Situation

Upright:
And the walls come tumbling down—in spite of all your best efforts, everything is crashing down around your ears. Hunker down and prepare for the worst.

Reversed:
You can open your eyes now; the major damage has already been done. Time to start picking up the pieces and figure out how it all went so very wrong.

Position 2—The Crossing

Upright:
You are on a collision course with a wall of epic proportions and it is going to leave a mark. Slow down; don't make things worse than they already are.

Reversed:
Not much more can be ruined at this point—time to start rebuilding. It wouldn't hurt to show a little gratitude for what you've still got, either.

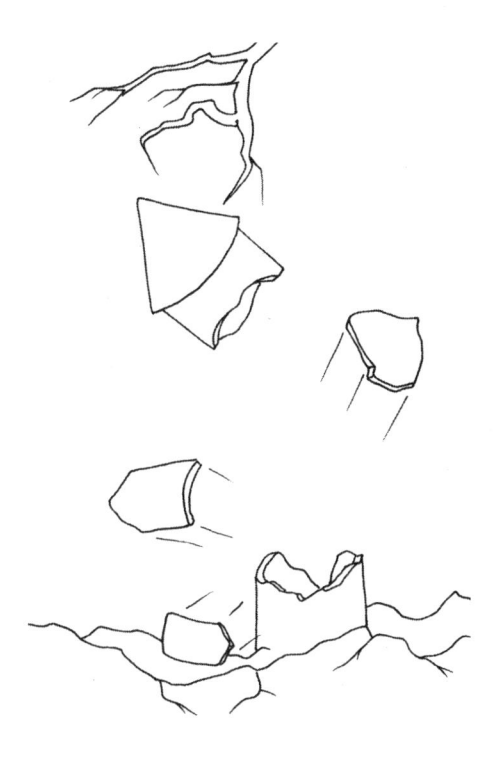

Position 3—The Base

Upright:
All your good intentions have brought you to naught—this is a catastrophe in the making. Shake yourself and wake up from the apathetic slump you have fallen into.

Reversed:
All is lost, but think of it as cleansing, rather than a brutal purging. It wasn't within your power to stop anyway, so try to put a good face on it.

Position 4—The Past

Upright:
As soon as you think you are defeated, you are. Your dreams were crushed, but slipping into deep depression over what was lost won't bring them back.

Reversed:
You are the phoenix that rose from the ashes of devastation, able to face and deal with the changes. Reinventing yourself shows you learned from your mistakes.

Position —The Crowning

Upright:
It may not be the end of the world as you know it, but it might be close. Time to re-evaluate the situation and come up with Plan B—fast.

Reversed:
Your intuition has been telling you the coming changes were inevitable for a while now. The pain won't last forever—odds are you'll live to fight another day.

Position 6—The Future

Upright:
You're headed down a dead-end street. There's bigger and badder than you lurking in the shadows, so lose the "I'm the best thing since sliced bread" attitude.

Reversed:
Get ready to wipe the slate clean and make a fresh start once the dust settles. It will be a little inconvenient, maybe even uncomfortable at first, but still doable.

Position 7—The Self

Upright:
No room for sissies—you need to be stronger than you currently are. Go dig around in the closet and find the backbone that you know is in there somewhere.

Reversed:
No matter which way you turn, you can't catch a fair break. Your problems are increasing, not decreasing. Lower your goals (for now) to something more attainable.

Position 8 —Outside Influences

Upright:
It's up to you to find the calm place when everyone around you is panicking. Don't get swept up by mass hysteria. Breathe, think, and act, not react.

Reversed:
You may have the heart of a rebel, but your oppressors don't share your dream to rise up righteous against the system, man. Listen for slander and false accusations.

Position 9

—Hopes and Fears

Upright:
You may be hoping for change to shake things up. A shock to the system is just what is needed to reestablish the status quo. Be careful what you wish for.

Reversed:
Cats usually land on their feet after a fall because they adjust in midair. Better get your damage control plan out now to cushion your rapid descent.

Position 10

—The Outcome

Upright:
That light at the end of the tunnel is a train, not a path to escape. It's going to be bad—real bad. Heed the warnings and turn back.

Reversed:
Yeah, it has all gone to hell in a hand basket. Even though your blocks got kicked over, the foundation is intact and with that you can rebuild.

17. The Star

In the aftermath of the Tower, a glimmer of hope appears on the horizon. The Star serves to remind us that no how dark the hour, dawn will indeed come again. Make a wish when you see this in a reading—you never know what could happen. Have a little faith that tomorrow will be a better, brighter day.

Meaning in a Nutshell:
Hope

Position 1—The Situation

Upright:
The first clue that the storm is over is the sighting of a single star. Better times are coming. Prepare to be inspired by the wealth of opportunities.

Reversed:
The storm isn't quite over. Your faith is needed for a little while longer. You've got some emotional challenges ahead, so keep any negativity in check.

Position 2
—The Crossing

Upright:
It might seem bad right now, but there are good things just around the corner. Keep the hope alive that present difficulties are just a temporary state of being.

Reversed:
Pessimism serves no one, least of all you. If a helping hand is being offered, take it. Don't squander offered resources just because you're too proud to accept charity.

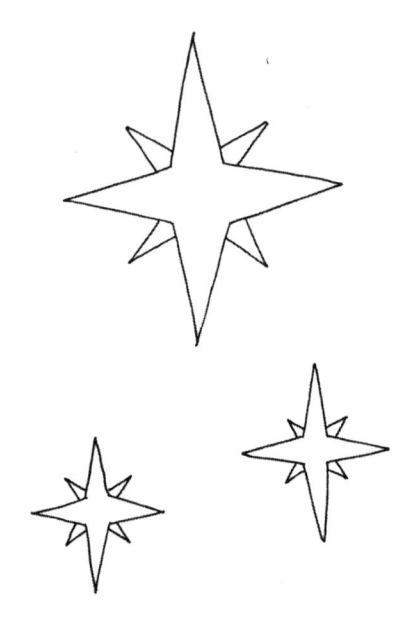

Position 3—The Base

Upright:
There is a new energy surrounding you and illuminating your path. Be at peace and bask in the serene knowledge that all is well and as it should be.

Reversed:
Closing your eyes and refusing to acknowledge the obvious won't help. You're expending your energy on a futile battle. Your negative vibes are only increasing the number of obstacles.

Position 4—The Past

Upright:
A beautiful day is dawning and a bright new sense of purpose appears on the horizon. Your faith that things would get better has served you well.

Reversed:
A loss of faith has brought an epiphany to your door. Your life scales are out of balance with unrealistic optimism on one side and a defeatist attitude on the other.

Position —The Crowning

Upright:
The day is resplendent with promise. If there's any healing to be done, you're off to a good start. Trust that you're being guided in the right direction.

Reversed:
The dream may have slipped out of your grasp for now. Don't take it personally—just pull yourself up and try again, perhaps with a little more humility.

Position 6—The Future

Upright:
If you're looking for a sign to proceed on your current action, this is it. Be open and receptive to new alternatives and above all, trust your intuition.

Reversed:
Delays and difficulties are rampant and aren't likely to get better. If you're running up against the same wall over and over, perhaps it's time to pick a new path.

Position 7—The Self

Upright:
Your inner strength, wisdom, and tact will give you that little something extra you need to succeed in attaining your goals. Being at peace with yourself is its own reward.

Reversed:
If you don't have faith in yourself, no one else will either. Ditto too much confidence without having proved yourself. Let your actions speak for themselves.

Position 8 —Outside Influences

Upright:
The souls around you are filled with love and offer their protection. You have their support in your endeavors, so an occasional thank you "just because" wouldn't hurt.

Reversed:
Superficiality only impresses those without the desire to look more closely to see things as they truly are. True friends are more interested in what is inside.

Position 9
—Hopes and Fears

Upright:
Pun intended, you have the potential to be a shining star in the dark night. You have bright expectations—just temper them with a bit of realism and you'll be fine.

Reversed:
Life is full of disappointment. It is how we deal with it that defines us. Constant complaining about what you cannot change is a waste of energy, so stop.

Position 10
—The Outcome

Upright:
You are filled with a new sense of purpose and the air simply sparkles with promise and potential. It's all looking good enough to eat—here's your fork.

Reversed:
So sad, so bad—all the wishing in the known universe isn't going to help this situation out. Don't feel sorry for yourself. Readjust your priorities or establish some news ones.

18. The Moon

Deep and mysterious, The Moon watches from above. Lovers swoon beneath it. Wolves howl at its stark beauty. It controls the tides, both of oceans and of our emotions. Bartenders and hospital emergency room staff will tell you it definitely affects us. Remember—things bathed in moonlight look a lot different in the harsh light of dawn.

Meaning in a Nutshell:
Illusions

Position 1—The Situation

Upright:
Posers and imposters lurk around every corner and there is deception afoot. Don't believe what you see. Chances are good that your perception is being distorted.

Reversed:
Yank the wool from over your eyes. You're being gifted with a rare moment of clarity—use it to shine some bright light into those unknown, lurking shadows.

Position 2
—The Crossing

Upright:
Not everything can be felt, seen, or touched, and you know there is a whole unseen world just waiting to be explored. Tread lightly until you get your bearings.

Reversed:
You may be on the receiving end of assistance or, at the very least, some useful information from a very unlikely source. Don't look a gift horse in the mouth.

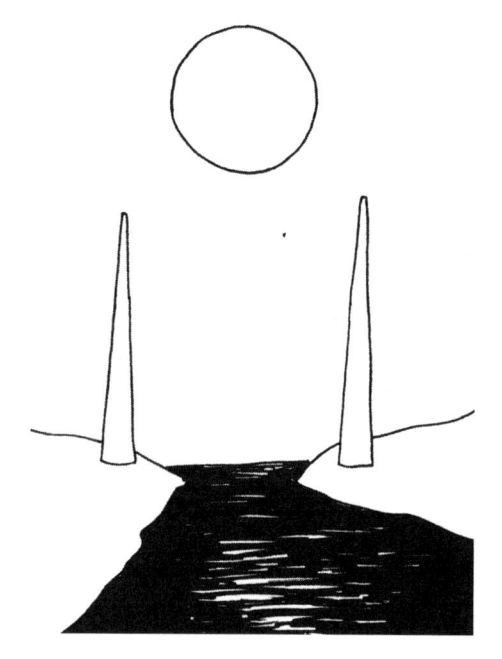

Position 3—The Base

Upright:
There is more to the story than meets the eye, so don't push forward without getting all the facts first. It may be best to maintain a low profile right now.

Reversed:
Hidden truths are exposed and the hard questions you've had are being answered. If anyone has been dishonest in their dealings, rest assured it's coming to light.

Position 4—The Past

Upright:
It's dodgy trying to find your way in the dark. You've got the bumps and scrapes to prove it. There's a lesson: make sure of your footing before you step.

Reversed:
Your eyes were opened and it may or may not have been painful. It was necessary, however, to get you and reality to hang out together for a while.

Position —The Crowning

Upright:
Oh, what a tangled web we weave...Sir Walter aside, there is mischief afoot. Someone's trying to pull a fast one and they could just get away with it if you're not watchful.

Reversed:
It's show time—the stage lights will be blazing on any second. If you're not in place, it's time to get there. All eyes will be on you.

Position 6—The Future

Upright:
The layers of deception are getting deeper and deeper. Certain you've made a mistake, you aren't quite sure how to go about correcting it. *Hubba hubba*—who do you trust?

Reversed:
Just like cockroaches in a kitchen, everyone not playing nice will scurry when the lights come on. Take particular notice who is watching the wall switches.

Position 7—The Self

Upright:
Being deceitful to others is bad enough, but lying to yourself is inexcusable. Make sure you understand not only your ulterior motives, but what also drives them.

Reversed:
It's a good time to start studying the occult arts if that is something that interests you. Get in touch with your spiritual side; it may be in need of your undivided attention.

Position 8 —Outside Influences

Upright:
Someone who has gained your trust is not being truthful with you. Beware of those who appear to be benign, because they may have other ideas and hidden agendas.

Reversed:
Don't tell everything you know as you may not be able to tell right away who your true friends are. You are vulnerable right now—lay low until this time passes.

Position 9
—Hopes and Fears

Upright:
You're afraid of being tricked, and rightfully so. The cunning recognize an easy mark when they see one. You're not seeing things for what they truly are: flawed.

Reversed:
They might try, but no one is going to get the upper hand without your permission. Be tactful in your words and deeds, give nothing away before you're ready.

Position 10
—The Outcome

Upright:
If there's no peephole, it's hard to tell who is on the other side of the door. Just because you act nobly and without guile, don't assume everyone else does, too.

Reversed:
If it's the naked truth you're after you're going to get it, warts and all. Try not to stare when everything gets put out in the open for all to see.

19. The Sun

Lay back and slip on those designer Oakleys—when you see The Sun in a reading, know that all is well in your world and life is golden. This is one of the two cards that traditionally has no reversed meaning, but reversals generally mean you'll have to wait a little longer for your poolside cabana chair and frozen drink.

Meaning in a Nutshell: Happiness

Position 1—The Situation

Upright:
Life is beautiful and everything is copacetic. It probably couldn't get any better if you tried, but don't let that stop you from opening your arms wider to embrace the goodness.

Reversed:
A little sunshine is a good thing, but don't forget your emotional sunscreen—if you're not careful you'll get burned out. Show a little extra gratitude for your blessings.

Position 2 —The Crossing

Upright:
If you're in a dark place, know the Sun is coming out to add a little warmth to your life. Good fortune is yours for the taking, smiling upon you and your endeavors.

Reversed:
The help you need is on the way; it's just taking the scenic route to get to you. Have faith and hold in there just a little while longer.

Position 3—The Base

Upright:
The current situation is grounded in positive energy and the sure knowledge that love surrounds you. It's a great feeling, knowing that everything is as it should be.

Reversed:
Lose the sense of entitlement. Don't take the good things in your life for granted. Be grateful for the gifts you've received and don't forget to say thanks.

Position 4—The Past

Upright:
Things have been going well for you up to this point. You got off to a good start and caught a lot of breaks along the way.

Reversed:
Perhaps it was ennui that got you moving, perhaps not. Either way, you grew dissatisfied with the status quo, wondering if perhaps there was more out there for you.

Position —The Crowning

Upright:
You've got all the potential for success, in the right place at the right time. You are centered and grounded, knowing what you want and how to get there.

Reversed:
You're on the right flight, just in coach instead of first class. Be patient and relax; good things are coming. Don't watch the pot—the water will boil on its own.

Position 6—The Future

Upright:
The good news you're waiting for is just around the corner. Get ready to get busy when it arrives—awesomeness is on the move. Don't forget to act surprised, though.

Reversed:
Some of the initial excitement may be wearing off and the trip is becoming humdrum and routine. Try to reclaim your original happiness and remember your motivation.

Position 7—The Self

Upright:
Self-love is a great thing—it allows you to be confident in your abilities, yet humble enough to know you can still improve. Your pride is well-deserved.

Reversed:
There's a thin line between confidence and conceit. You've still got a lot of lessons to learn, but the first step in learning is acknowledging how much you don't know.

Position 8 —Outside Influences

Upright:
If you've got favors owed that can help you, now is the time to call them in. Don't be afraid to ask for a boost up the ladder from those willing to assist.

Reversed:
Take time for yourself. You cannot be all things to all people, no matter how hard you try. Your vast energy sources will be drained dry if you're careful.

Position 9
—Hopes and Fears
Upright:
Of course you want things to go the way you want—it is human nature. Make your wishes for the highest good of all concerned and let it go at that.

Reversed:
Sometimes the building anticipation is half the fun of the trip itself. Don't be in such a rush—everything will come together when it's good and damn well ready. Quit stressing.

Position 10
—The Outcome
Upright:
Just like the saying goes—it's all good. If you're looking for an answer, this is a positive response to your question. Yours is truly a charmed life.

Reversed:
Don't' get disappointed or discouraged if what you want doesn't materialize right away. It may be a good to examine what you're after to see if it's worth all the effort.

20. Judgment

You know the old saying "your day will come"? Well, today is that day — all your hard work (or lack thereof) will be on display for the whole world to see. Better hope all the *t*'s were crossed and *i*'s dotted — this is a pass/fail exam and there aren't any retakes. No quarter given, so don't bother asking for leniency.

Meaning in a Nutshell: Karma

Position 1—The Situation

Upright:
The day of reckoning has arrived and it is time to find out if all of your past efforts were successful or not. There is no turning back now.

Reversed:
Last minute cramming for finals isn't going to help you now. You've been caught totally unprepared, wasting the available opportunities to study. Change is coming up fast.

Position 2 —The Crossing

Upright:
If you were hoping for a new cycle to emerge, you are in luck. The current status quo is drawing to a close—the old king is dead, long live the new king.

Reversed:
You are going against what you know in your heart to be right and this will lead to nothing good. Take the blinders off and look at the big picture.

Position 3—The Base

Upright:
This is the card of Karma and life changing decisions. It's time to pay those dues you keep hearing about and get ready to move forward.

Reversed:
All of your well-laid plans are coming to naught, and you are primarily responsible for their downfall. Your negative attitude and stubbornness isn't helping matters, either.

Position 4—The Past

Upright:
You've had a spiritual awakening in your not-so-recent past that caused you to first question, then make some hard decisions about your future.

Reversed:
Things are going to change around you, whether you want them to or not. Living in a state of fear isn't living at all—it is prolonging the anxiety of the unknown.

Position —The Crowning

Upright:
This is a rite of passage and you are being transformed and molded into the person you are meant to be. Might be a little uncomfortable at first, but you'll adjust.

Reversed:
You're fighting a losing battle, so go with the flow rather than fighting the current to swim upstream. Holding tightly to a grudge isn't good for you or the grudge.

Position 6—The Future

Upright:
If there is someone you want to reconcile with, now might be the time. Admit and repent from prior bad acts, then release them. Free yourself from guilt.

Reversed:
Remember building sand castles at the beach, then watching the tide come in, destroying all your hard work? Choose your next building spot with more forethought for the future.

Position 7—The Self

Upright:
Self-improvement starts from within. Take stock of who you are and who you want to be; then map out the necessary steps to get there. Seek your destiny.

Reversed:
Confusion reigns—where to go, what to do, and oh, look at what a fine mess you've gotten yourself into. Don't let disappointment sour your outlook on life.

Position 8 —Outside Influences

Upright:
Those around you are supportive and will give you the necessary space to flex your burgeoning muscles if you ask politely. Remember to play by the rules, though.

Reversed:
Those around you may not only be inhospitable, but downright cold. You can't expect to have friends if you haven't been one in return. Quid pro quo, Clarice.

Position 9
—Hopes and Fears
Upright:
It's all coming down to the wire, but not to fear—you've done your due diligence and are prepared for the judgment to be handed down. Resolution is imminent.

Reversed:
Any pending decisions will not be in your favor. Better start working on Plan B while you have the chance. Don't let any more opportunities be wasted.

Position 10
—The Outcome
Upright:
You take a great deal of pride in yourself, but it is well deserved—you've earned every single wrinkle, bump, and scar. Move forward knowing you did it right.

Reversed:
Guard against seeing only what you wish to see. Remember that the lessons unlearned are those you are doomed to repeat over and over and over.

21. The World

The last card in the Major Arcana, The World indicates completion, a graduation of sorts. This part of your journey is drawing to a close so that the new cycle can begin. Take a moment to pause and reflect upon your successes because you worked hard to get where you are. Great job—now get ready to face your next challenge head on.

**Meaning in a Nutshell:
Achievement**

Position 1—The Situation

Upright:
You are coming into a new cycle in your life, one of empowerment and promise, and you spark with creative fire. Channel that energy into something awesome.

Reversed:
All you want is just one chance to show the world how competent you can be. Dreams are great, but don't forget to keep working hard in the meantime.

Position 2

—The Crossing

Upright:
There may be travel or relocation in the works. If a change of scenery is offered, take it. This is a conducive atmosphere for you to learn from your surroundings.

Reversed:
You see yourself as the initiate, bright-eyed and bushy-tailed, ready to tackle the world. Not so fast—slow down and get some more information before you take off.

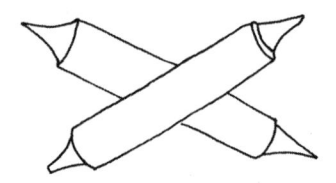

Position 3—The Base

Upright:
Goals have been reached and the bells of triumph are ringing. If it is possible to achieve perfection, you're as close as you can get at this moment.

Reversed:
Thing are not going quite as fast as you'd like, but don't lose heart and get distracted by an unrealistic time schedule. There may be business left unfinished.

Position 4—The Past

Upright:
You deserve a pat on the back, because your past successes have you to thank for bringing them into being! Props to you for reaching your goals.

Reversed:
Tie game...two seconds on the clock...he shoots...he scores! Home team wins! You didn't see it though; you left for the parking lot thinking the game was over. Reexamine past priorities.

Position —The Crowning

Upright:
The recognition you seek will be yours and success is assured. Your dreams are finally becoming reality and there is nothing left to do but kick back and enjoy the ride.

Reversed:
Fear of failure is no excuse for failing to attempt. If you want the fruit badly enough, be prepared to go out on the limb to get it.

Position 6—The Future

Upright:
After a lot of soul searching, you have decided to take your first step on the new path that you have chosen. All the loose ends are tied up (or soon will be).

Reversed:
You may feel as if you're always chasing rainbows, but you're making more progress than you know. Widen your scope—are you dreaming big enough? Watch spending.

Position 7—The Self

Upright:
Admittedly, you might not have felt it sometimes, but you always carry an air of calm competency about you. You appreciate your victories because you worked hard for them.

Reversed:
Resisting change doesn't do anything except slow down your Karmic growth. Suck it up and take your medicine—it goes down better with a sweet, not bitter, attitude.

Position 8 —Outside Influences

Upright:
Your light shines so brightly you can't help but pull in admirers and fans. You've earned the respect and accolades you're getting. Be humble, but guard against false modesty.

Reversed:
Indulging in self-sabotage is no way to go through life—there are too many people willing to do that for you. Have confidence in your abilities and ignore the critics.

Position 9
—Hopes and Fears

Upright:
Your expertise and acumen has led you to the position you are in now. Enjoy your moment in the sun, then move on to the next phase of your life.

Reversed:
You're not quite ready to close the book on this part of your life—there are too many remaining loose ends. Take care of the small things before they become big things.

Position 10
—The Outcome

Upright:
Epic WIN! It's all you, it's all now, and it's all good. Think of yourself as a conduit of the Universe and allow its wisdom and knowledge to flow.

Reversed:
While your shining moment is definitely on the horizon, it's not here yet. There are unavoidable delays, obstacles, and roadblocks left to get past. Refocus on your goals.

The Minors

Swords

The Ace of Swords

Aces translate into Ones and Ones are always beginnings. Involving communication and conflict, Swords are also related to health issues. If you're not taking care of yourself, their appearance in a reading could be bearing an important hidden message.

Meaning in a Nutshell:
Initiation

Position 1—The Situation

Upright:
Lines of communication are opening up. There may be legal activity on the horizon—either way, expect things to start moving quickly.

Reversed:
The energy exerted is misguided and misdirected. There is confusion as to who is in charge, what is being done and why.

Position 2—The Crossing

Upright:
You are on the right side in this conflict and aligned with the winning team. The timing is right to make your move.

Reversed:
Someone is being too heavy handed and their empty use of force will come to nothing. Don't allow yourself be bullied.

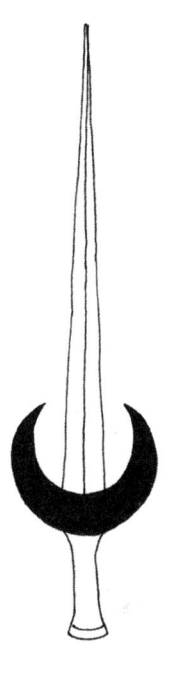

Position 3—The Base

Upright:
A long anticipated battle has arrived, and the call to arms has been raised. The time to strike the first blow is now.

Reversed:
Destructive forces are at work, and will bring nothing but confusion and doubt at best, violence and threats at the worst.

Position 4—The Past

Upright:
You seized the opportunity placed before you and were prepared to accept the consequences. Your goals were reasonable.

Reversed:
Any personal power you had was ripped unceremoniously from you and that may be responsible for the chip on your shoulder.

Position —The Crowning

Upright:
You have the leadership skills to take the reins. Speak clearly and others will listen. Act, and set the example to follow.

Reversed:
Power—you're doing it wrong. Tyranny, heavy-handed tactics and domination will win you nothing but more enemies.

Position 6—The Future

Upright:
An opportunity for conquest and victory will be coming up soon—prepare now to take full advantage of it.

Reversed:
You are directing others to do your dirty work, and given the chance, they will turn on you in a heartbeat.

Position 7—The Self

Upright:
You are idealistic, believing that conviction will be your shield and truth your sword. You temper your strength through adversity and welcome challenge.

Reversed:
You are using your power without regard for those it impacts. Your personal opinion isn't automatically the right one.

Position 8—Outside Influences

Upright:
Those around you will stand at your side if you go to battle. Appreciate them; they are the ones watching your back.

Reversed:
Sorry, you're on your own this time. The expected help isn't coming. Your struggle will be an uphill one.

Position 9

—Hopes and Fears

Upright:
You may be ready to wield your authority and lead the charge. The timing is right to fight for what you believe in.

Reversed:
You are in fear of anticipated punishment, either deserved or unwarranted. Be careful whose words you take to heart.

Position 10

—The Outcome

Upright:
Yours is a righteous battle so bolster your resolve. Make your long term goals then prepare to act to make them real.

Reversed:
You have acted without thinking things through. Sometimes it is best to run away and live to fight another day.

The Two of Swords

You may have firmly decided to remain ambivalent…or not. This Two is related to decision making, so if you're swaying this way and that on the subject, it's time to make up your mind about how you really feel.

Meaning in a Nutshell:
Indecision

Position 1—The Situation

Upright:
Ignoring the problem won't make it go away; in fact, your indecision may make it worse than it really needs to be.

Reversed:
When you first take off the blindfold, give your eyes time to adjust before you leap into action.

Position 2—The Crossing

Upright:
You're got some personal drama, or perhaps you're being drawn into someone else's. Either way, there's some intrigue going on.

Reversed:
There are some new ideas floating around that could really change the way you think. Open your mind a crack.

Position 3—The Base

Upright:
You have reached an impasse—nobody is budging from their opinion or giving an inch towards a needed compromise.

Revrsed:
The treachery you have been suspecting is finally being exposed. Give yourself credit for being so alert.

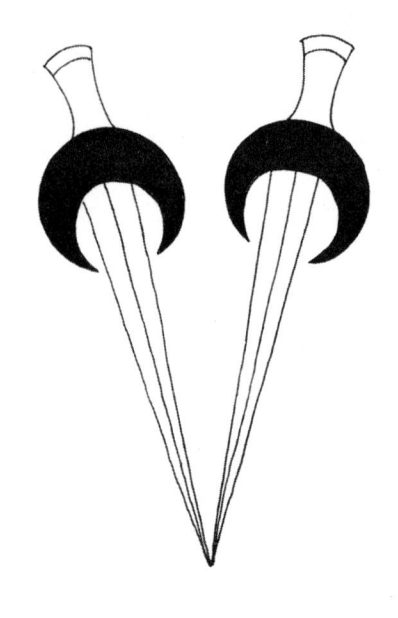

Position 4—The Past

Upright:
You have long pretended there wasn't an elephant in the living room. Nice to meet you Cleopatra, Queen of *De-nial*.

Reversed:
Your initiative in taking charge has served you well in heading off an unpleasant, if not unavoidable situation.

Position —The Crowning

Upright:
You have reached a stalemate in your situation. Best find a solution you can tolerate, unless you change courses altogether.

Reversed:
Breaking out of the state you're in takes courage, but you're going to have to be the one to make the first move.

Position 6—The Future

Upright:
Refusing to acknowledge the problem doesn't make it any less real. You run the risk of looking just plain silly about it.

Reversed:
You can't always just pick up your toys and go home when the other kids don't play nice. Learn to share.

Position 7—The Self

Upright:
You're straddling the fence, refusing to lean one way or the other. Stop worrying so much about what everyone else is thinking.

Reversed:
Your mind is finally set, so suit up and get ready for some action. Put your game face on, Tiger.

Position 8 —Outside Influences

Upright:
If you need another opinion, don't look to your friends for your motivation. They are as noncommittal as you are.

Reversed:
Be careful who persuades you over to their line of thinking. Don't believe anything without doing all your homework, regardless of the source.

Position 9 —Hopes and Fears

Upright:
Nothing is going to get done unless someone decides to give a little; and honestly, the odds aren't good at this rate.

Reversed:
Ready or not, change is upon you. Embrace the fresh energy and be ready to strike while the iron is hot.

Position 10 —The Outcome

Upright:
It is critical that you strike a balance between the opposing forces in your life. Pick an opinion and stick with it.

Reversed:
You're being inundated on all sides with false information. Make sure of your facts—and their sources—before acting.

The Three of Swords

Three is a number of growth, but in the Suit of Swords it's a painful lesson on how and who to trust with your feelings. This card teaches you how to confront your pain, face it head on, and learn from it.

Meaning in a Nutshell:
Betrayal

Position 1—The Situation

Upright:
There's no getting around it—the situation is fraught with heartbreaking, bone-aching angst. Remember the song "Love Stinks"? Yeah, it's that bad.

Reversed:
You're moving into the recovery portion of your evening. Now is the time to start checking your heart and ego for damage.

Position 2 —The Crossing

Upright:
Someone has done you wrong. Regardless of who is in the right, you are the one feeling the weight of the unexpected betrayal.

Reversed:
Tensions are running high and there is discord with those you love, or at least like enough to be around.

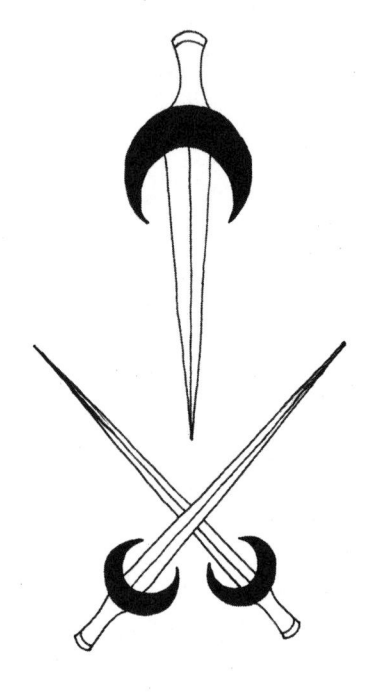

Position 3—The Base

Upright:
There has been some serious upheaval of late. It chafes you to no end that you didn't see this one coming.

Reversed:
You've had the prerequisite feeling sorry for yourself period; now it is time to move on and get on with living.

Position 4—The Past

Upright:
There has been pain in the past, so much so that the mere memory of it shadows the present.

Reversed:
You aren't just revisiting the past; you bought property there. Dredging up ancient history isn't helping anyone, least of all you.

Position

—The Crowning

Upright:
You may not like it, but perhaps time apart from the situation is what is needed now. Step back a little.

Reversed:
There is an emotional distance at this time. Maybe time heals all. Or maybe it doesn't. You'll need to wait and see.

Position 6—The Future

Upright:
All references to Winger aside, you are headed for a heartache in a big kind of way. There is stormy emotional weather ahead.

Reversed:
Don't dwell on the immediate pain. Suck it up and deal for now, you can sort out the details later.

Position 7—The Self

Upright:
You are experiencing a great deal of sorrow, up to and including the feeling that the world will never turn the same way again.

Reversed:
Over your head in Self Pity Lake, you wouldn't admit you're hurting for anything—or anyone—in the world.

Position 8

—Outside Influences

Upright:
There's a lot of negativity in the air; others have their own drama to deal with and can't be bothered with yours.

Reversed:
Shoulders to cry on are in short supply right now. Better that you rely on yourself for this crisis.

Position 9

—Hopes and Fears

Upright:
Beware: someone is not presenting an honest face to you and they do not have your best interests at heart.

Reversed:
You will live. It will get better. It could be time to spend some quality time with just yourself.

Position 10

—The Outcome

Upright:
Beware of lovers who make promises with their fingers crossed behind their backs, for they cannot be trusted to keep your business off YouTube.

Reversed:
Don't fall for the "I was weak" line. You can't be tempted into naughtiness if you weren't interested in the first place.

The Four of Swords

Sometimes you want to take a break; sometimes you are forced to. Use the time wisely to recharge your batteries or give your plans and ideas further thought. Fours are a number of rest and rejuvenation, so take advantage of the lull.

Meaning in a Nutshell:
Rest

Position 1—The Situation

Upright:
Time to relax and rejuvenate, recuperate if necessary, think the deep thoughts you've been putting off. You've got time.

Reversed:
Nothing will move until it is good and damn ready. If patience isn't one of your virtues, there's no better time to work on it.

Position 2 —The Crossing

Upright:
Put everything on hold and go into hibernation mode. Disconnect for a while to get your head back on straight.

Reversed:
There is no snooze button on this alarm clock—it's time to get up and get moving. You've slept long enough.

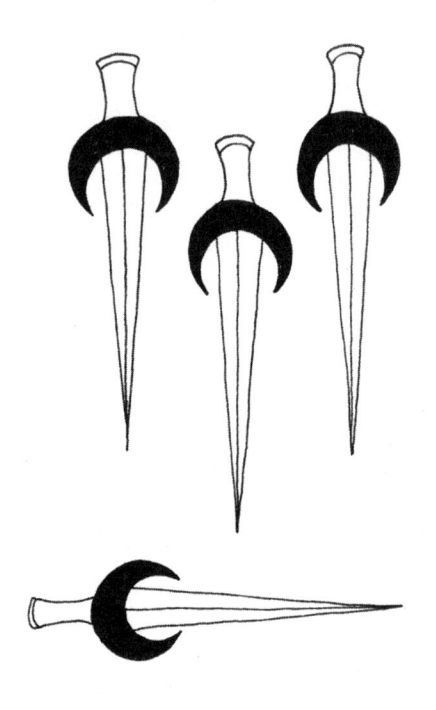

Position 3—The Base

Upright:
You're being forced into a period of inactivity. No use fighting it; your energy could be better spent elsewhere.

Reversed:
Get ready to rouse from your recent dormancy. The time for words is over. Action is what is needed now.

Position 4—The Past

Upright:
Sometimes withdrawing from the world is what the heart and mind need to stay intact. It's not always a bad thing.

Reversed:
Something kicked you into gear. Remember how good it felt to finally be doing something about your problems instead of just talking.

Position —The Crowning

Upright:
You're on the road to recovery. Don't rush the healing process— the worse the pain, the longer it takes to feel better.

Reversed:
If you plan anything at this time, prepare for it to take longer than expected. Nothing is going according to schedule.

Position 6—The Future

Upright:
Before you open your mouth, think about what's coming out. Think twice about potential consequences. Pause and reflect before you act.

Reversed:
If the fire is going out, now is the time to rekindle those desires. If you want to reconnect with someone, go for it.

Position 7—The Self

Upright:
There's a possible illness or period of convalescence—if you don't take care of yourself first, you can't take care of others.

Reversed:
Don't let resentment over what you don't think you have enough of make you bitter. If you don't the way things are, change them.

Position 8 —Outside Influences

Upright:
There could be work-related difficulties. Don't be surprised if people mistake you for the complaints desk. Let it roll off.

Reversed:
It's rejoin society time, so make yourself a little more visible. Speak up and don't shrink away from the attention.

Position 9 —Hopes and Fears

Upright:
You can pretend it was your idea to take time off. It wasn't, though. A little inner contemplation would do you good.

Reversed:
Don't worry about lagging behind—you're going to bounce back bigger and better than ever. Just be patient.

Position 10 —The Outcome

Upright:
Heave a big sigh of relief; it is time to take a break from strife. Rest and live to fight another day.

Reversed:
Welcome back—the world has missed you. Time to get back into the swing of things and recapture the delicious rush of living.

The Five of Swords

Five is a number of transition—when connected with Swords, it makes for a bumpy ride. Whether you're the wolf in sheep's clothing or a paper tiger, perception is everything. The moment you think you've lost, you have.

**Meaning in a Nutshell:
Humiliation**

Position 1—The Situation

Upright:
The balance of power is a precarious thing. Right now, it's tilting away from you and treachery is afoot—tread lightly.

Reversed:
If you're hoping for vindication, you're in the right place. The playing field is getting ready to even out.

Position 2—The Crossing

Upright:
Your best laid plans are falling to ruin. Someone is out to sabotage your efforts and you may not see them coming.

Reversed:
Don't let jealousy goad you into doing something you'll regret. Harsh words can't be called back once they've left your lips.

Position 3—The Base

Upright:
You're not going to make any friends along the way if you run roughshod over everyone you meet.

Reversed:
The words "neener, neener" take on new meaning depending on which side you're on. Don't be in such a rush to gloat.

Position 4—The Past

Upright:
It's never fun to be the object of gossip. Doesn't matter if what they're saying is true or not; it still stings.

Reversed:
You went spoiling for a fight and got more than you bargained for. Be more careful who you pick on next time.

Position
—The Crowning

Upright:
It's great to be on the winning team, but don't compromise yourself in the pursuit of glory. It's not worth it.

Reversed:
You're got just as much right as anyone to follow your dreams. Don't let anyone bully you into thinking you don't.

Position 6—The Future

Upright:
Don't go looking for trouble—it'll find you. You need to accept your fair share of blame for the current mess.

Reversed:
Mind your business and don't go poking around in things not of your concern. Now isn't the time to be the world police.

Position 7—The Self

Upright:
You'd do well to remember that you're not the only one affected by your actions. Don't let spitefulness cloud your judgment.

Reversed:
Don't let low self-esteem cause you to agree to something you wouldn't do otherwise. You don't need anyone's approval.

Position 8
—Outside Influences

Upright:
Someone in your midst isn't who or what they claim to be. Be careful to whom you give personal information.

Reversed:
Don't look for sympathetic ears or spare shoulders to cry on in your immediate vicinity. People are less tolerant than usual.

Position 9
—Hopes and Fears

Upright:
You might be the one on stage, but someone else is pulling your strings. Who is the boss of you and why?

Reversed:
If you have been falsely accused, an acquittal is possible. See, you were right all along to have acted as you did.

Position 10
—The Outcome

Upright:
There isn't much that will turn people off faster than a graceless winner, causing resentment rather than the admiration you desire.

Reversed:
You have come out on top and won fair and square by taking the high road instead of relying on underhanded methods.

The Six of Swords

The winds of change have blown you into smoother waters and you can breathe easy again. Enjoy the scenery and catch your breath; you're overdue for a little R&R. Harmony and cooler heads once again prevail—for now.

Meaning in a Nutshell:
Peace

Position 1—The Situation

Upright:
Turbulent waves have stopped rocking your boat; time to surrender the helm and let someone else do the driving for a while.

Reversed:
Don't get lulled into a false sense of security. Better fasten your seatbelts—it's going to be a bumpy night.

Position 2—The Crossing

Upright:
Keep an open mind and toss your preconceived notions out the window. Time to look for new solutions to old problems.

Reversed:
You wanted change, but it might not be exactly as you'd hoped. Next time, be more specific in what you want.

Position 3—The Base

Upright:
You've reached a turning point. It's time to make some decisions about where you go from here.

Reversed:
Times are about to get hard. Ignoring your problems doesn't make them go away—it makes correcting them take longer.

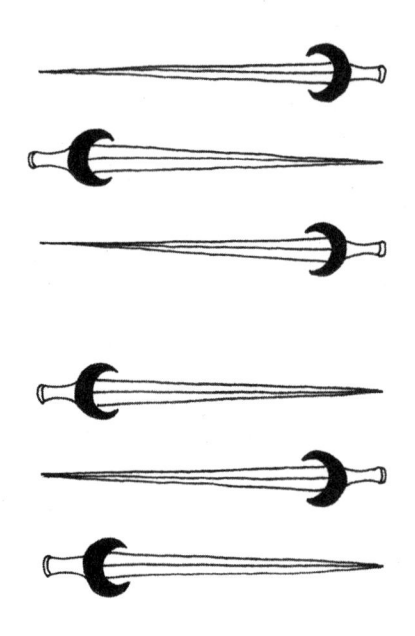

Position 4—The Past

Upright:
Some of your past behaviors have been questionable, a few downright destructive. Good that you've been able to rise above them.

Reversed:
Saving time is a good thing, but taking too many shortcuts makes for unfavorable compromises and poor quality.

Position
—The Crowning

Upright:
Your journey thus far left marks on your spirit but don't let numbness overwhelm you. Take some time to rejuvenate.

Reversed:
This is a safe harbor, but does your ship need to be sheltered or to brave the unfamiliar seas towards your goal?

Position 6
—The Future

Upright:
There's no reason why you can't blow off some steam. Do it in a controlled environment—play hard, but carefully.

Reversed:
No, it's not your imagination playing tricks. Things are starting to heat up and tensions are ratcheting up a notch.

Position 7—The Self

Upright:
Practical and sensible, you are not one to rock the boat, preferring to maintain a low profile and out of the limelight.

Reversed:
Swimming against the current is a good way to wear yourself out. Don't you have better uses for all that energy?

Position 8
—Outside Influences

Upright:
It's good to have a safety net of family/friends to fall back on, but don't become dependent on it.

Reversed:
Don't worry about feeling left out—you're going to have all the attention you can handle, most of it unwanted.

Position 9
—Hopes and Fears

Upright:
All you want is a little bit of peace and quiet—is that too much to ask? You may have unexpected visitors.

Reversed:
There may be an unpleasant turn of events. Not quite worst-case-scenario type stuff, but definitely not something you wanted to happen.

Position 10
—The Outcome

Upright:
This is the calm after the storm. Take a well-earned rest knowing you're going to catch a break for a while.

Reversed:
This is the eye of the hurricane; there is still more of the storm to navigate in your search for peaceful waters.

The Seven of Swords

There is mischief afoot and not the fun kind—this is the sort that starts wars. You don't get to pick and choose the rules you want to abide by. Lying, cheating, and stealing is a dangerous way to go through life.

Meaning in a Nutshell:
Sabotage

Position 1—The Situation

Upright:
Ooh, somebody's got a dirty little secret. There's a whole lot of covering up and covering tracks going on. Be on guard.

Reversed:
Full disclosure means everyone has to show all the cards they are holding. Full doesn't mean willingly, though.

Position 2—The Crossing

Upright:
Secure your valuables and watch who you share your words with—thievery takes all kinds of shapes and forms.

Reversed:
There isn't much following through to finish what has already been started. There is still time to redeem yourself.

Position 3—The Base

Upright:
Instigating problems may come back to bite you. Don't use it as a diversion to keep eyes from what you're doing.

Reversed:
Don't get so obsessed with the idea of payback you lose sight of what is really important: moving forward.

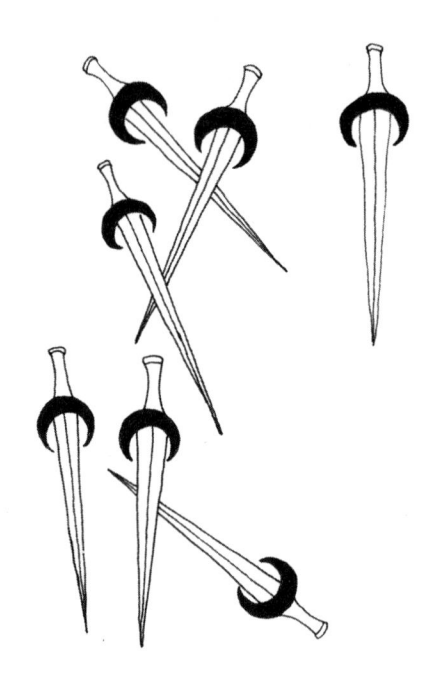

Position 4—The Past

Upright:
You can talk yourself into just about anything, and have. Impulsive actions have landed you in hot water.

Reversed:
Giving up without a fight shows how little confidence you have in your own abilities. Who is that helping in the long run?

Position
—The Crowning

Upright:
It's just bad news all the way around and everyone is wildly pointing fingers. Accept your share of the responsibility.

Reversed:
Condescension is a bad habit. Even if you do think you're better than everyone else, keep it to yourself.

Position 6—The Future

Upright:
There may be some upcoming legal issues. Don't stick your head in the sand—lawyer up and face the coming challenge head on.

Reversed:
It wouldn't hurt to exercise a little prudence and discretion. Hear the full argument before you act or react.

Position 7—The Self

Upright:
That uncomfortable feeling is called guilt. You have it because you have a conscience and know what you did was wrong.

Reversed:
Don't make assumptions based on partial knowledge or overcompensate for what you feel you don't have. Patience, young Grasshopper.

Position 8
—Outside Influences

Upright:
If you refuse to take good advice, don't whine when you get in deeper trouble. Admitting you don't know everything is the first step.

Reversed:
Your critics are not just trying to tear you down—they might be trying to help you get better. Listen.

Position 9
—Hopes and Fears

Upright:
Someone is distorting the truth. It's up to you to locate the deception before it is too late. Stay alert.

Reversed:
Open up and say *AH!* It's time to take the medicine you've been putting off. The sooner it's done, the sooner it's over.

Position 10
—The Outcome

Upright:
There is a fly in your ointment, even if he/she hasn't shown their face yet. Your plans are in danger of sabotage.

Reversed:
It's not as bad as it looks, although it's pretty bad. Stolen property may find its way home again.

The Eight of Swords

It's bad enough being held captive, worse yet to discover you are your own jailer. Others have power over you only to the extent that you allow it. Eight is the number of independence — get yourself some and lose the helpless act.

Meaning in a Nutshell:
Imprisonment

Position 1—The Situation

Upright:
Does your prison look familiar? Yep, you made it. You are held captive by your own words and deeds.

Reversed:
Breaking free is an equal test of emotion and will. You've seen the problem and how to fix it — now get moving.

Position 2
—The Crossing

Upright:
For whatever reason, you're holding yourself back. Maybe it's lack of resources or confidence. There are more options than you think.

Reversed:
The obstacles you dreaded most are being removed. Time for the "where do I go from here" discussion.

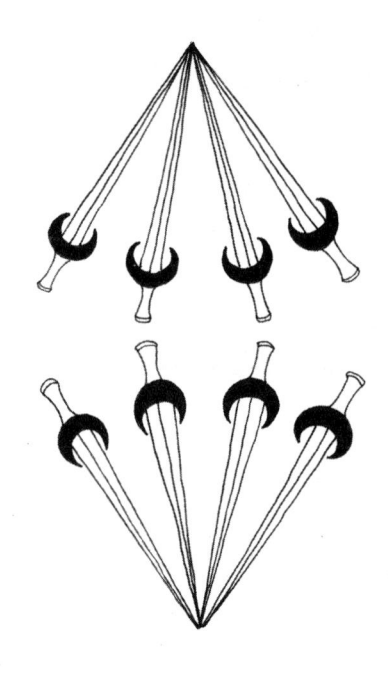

Position 3—The Base

Upright:
Your fear and indecision are keeping you in an unpleasant situation. It's not going to get better until you make it so.

Reversed:
An honest reevaluation of circumstances is in order — make sure you're not overdramatizing the problems to get the sympathy vote.

Position 4—The Past

Upright:
Your past environment was oppressive to say the least. It's no wonder you find yourself in same situation now. Déjà vu much?

Reversed:
There were those intent on keeping you down, but you dug deep and found the strength to make the needed changes.

Position —The Crowning

Upright:
You feel alone, trapped, and powerless to help yourself. With that mindset, you are. If you can't accept it, change it.

Reversed:
It's been rough going. You are moving into a time of relaxation after the dust settles from the recent stress.

Position 6—The Future

Upright:
Be very careful. The door you're going through is going to lock behind you. Make sure of your exits before taking your seat.

Reversed:
Your self confidence is coming back with a vengeance and you are a force to be reckoned with. *BOO-YAH!*

Position 7—The Self

Upright:
The frustration is getting to you and the more you ignore it, the worst it will get. It's time to face the truth.

Reversed:
This is a trial by fire, but you are up to the task. Shake off the heavy depression clouding your judgment.

Position 8 —Outside Influences

Upright:
Those around you are just fine with the status quo. You won't make any friends by shaking it up with new ideas.

Reversed:
Your support network is pushing you out of the nest so that you can learn to fly. It's tough love, but love nonetheless.

Position 9 —Hopes and Fears

Upright:
The damsel in distress needs a Plan B in case Prince Charming doesn't show. Why don't you get to work on that?

Reversed:
Freedom to be what and who you want is your greatest desire. It's up to you to take your power back.

Position 10 —The Outcome

Upright:
When you've got more restrictions than liberties, it's time to rethink your position. There has to be a better way.

Reversed:
You're moving on up to a better situation. Leave the past where it belongs—behind you. Look forward to a shiny future.

The Eight of Swords

The Nine of Swords

Ghoulies and ghosties and things that go bump in the night — our imagination plays tricks on us. The unknown is way scarier than the known. This Nine is a card of intellect — use yours and don't make things worse than they are.

Meaning in a Nutshell:
Anxiety

Position 1—The Situation

Upright:
Sleepless nights, days filled with worry and all kinds of "what if" scenarios — sound familiar? Your mind is working overtime.

Reversed:
Now is the darkness before the dawn, but make no mistake — dawn is coming. Worry changes nothing except the number of gray hairs.

Position 2 —The Crossing

Upright:
You've got your suspicions but don't jump to conclusions just yet — wait a while to see how things play out first.

Reversed:
It's time to clean house, starting with the attic. Get rid of those old ghosts and emotional baggage hanging about.

Position 3—The Base

Upright:
Up to your eyebrows in desperate anxiety, it seems everything is going wrong. Stop. Breathe. Now how bad is it really?

Reversed:
Facing your fears head on is a good way to send them packing. Hint: this requires courage on your part.

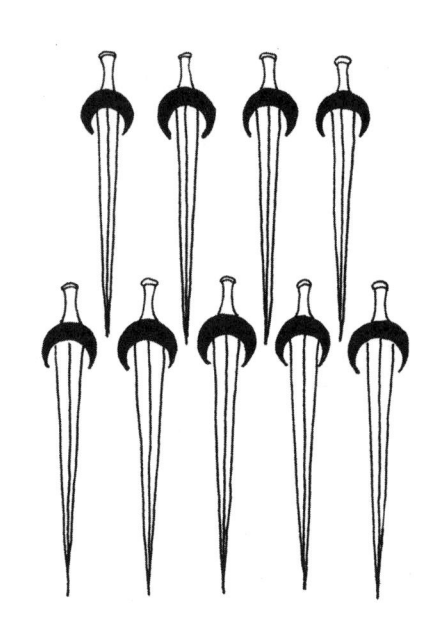

Position 4—The Past

Upright:
Depression has left its mark on you. You know what it is like to be isolated in your own personal hell, imagining the worst.

Reversed:
You may have overreacted a bit, but managed to pull yourself together. It's very stressful being freaked out all the time.

Position

—The Crowning

Upright:
Any promise made can be broken if given the right incentive — keep that in mind when your expectations outgrow the reality.

Reversed:
The process of recovery is slow, but healing. Focus on getting yourself well and releasing old hurts and disappointments.

Position 6—The Future

Upright:
Your nightmares are getting worse and it's only a matter of time before you either crack or confront them outright.

Reversed:
Your dreams are vivid. Write them down if you need to because they're trying to tell you something important.

Position 7—The Self

Upright:
Rather than talking about your problems, you internalize them, making them even worse. Talk about it. Troubles shared are troubles halved.

Reversed:
You can go to sleep with a clear conscience. Whatever went down, you know you did the right thing for all concerned.

Position 8

—Outside Influences

Upright:
Don't let mob hysteria dictate your actions. Think calmly and ask yourself if it's real or just the excitement talking.

Reversed:
It's going to take work to restore you to your previous glory, but you have supporters willing to help with your rehabilitation.

Position 9

—Hopes and Fears

Upright:
Negative energy draws only more negative energy. Lather, rinse, repeat — break the nonproductive worry chain now before it gets worse.

Reversed:
If you've been under the weather, you can look for healing energy to soon fill your life. Let your mind rest awhile.

Position 10

—The Outcome

Upright:
The nightmare isn't over yet. Don't dwell on *could be* — fear of a thing is usually worse than the thing itself.

Reversed:
Those first rays of light give you hope that dawn is here. You can relax knowing the worst is behind you.

The Nine of Swords

The Ten of Swords

Yes, it is as bad as it looks. The upside is there really isn't anywhere to go from here but up. Ten indicate the end of a cycle, but remember that every ending in a new beginning in disguise.

**Meaning in a Nutshell:
Inevitability**

Position 1—The Situation

Upright:
All resistance to the inevitable change is futile. You have fought your battle and lost. It's over now. Done.

Reversed:
You can come out now; the worst is over. Time to start cleaning up the mess and see what can be salvaged.

Position 2—The Crossing

Upright:
The advice you were given was bad and resulted in complete and utter devastation. Everything is crashing and burning around you.

Reversed:
All the unpleasant remnants and reminders are being swept away and it is time for a fresh start. Forgive yourself.

Position 3—The Base

Upright:
Welcome to Rock Bottom—population: you. The feeling of desolation is tangible. Good news is it has to get better from here.

Reversed:
There's nothing more to do here but embrace the future with optimism. There could be travel once you get your second wind.

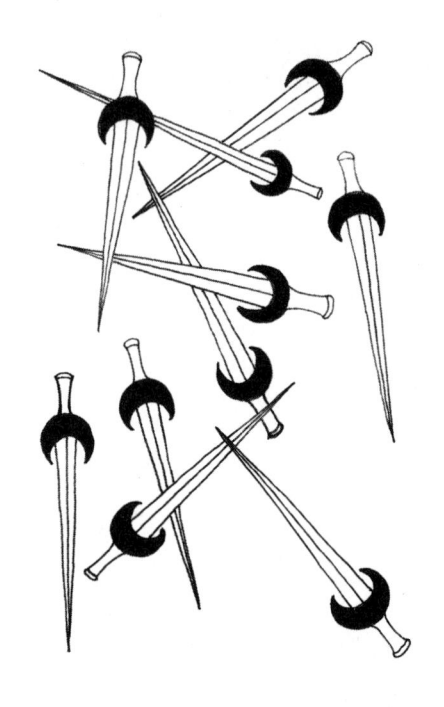

Position 4—The Past

Upright:
The whole thing was headed to hell in a hand basket anyway. Ignoring it didn't change anything.

Reversed:
You're no stranger to pain and heartbreak, but you have learned the lesson they both teach—resilience and self-acceptance.

Position —The Crowning

Upright:
Much of the pain you feel is self-inflicted from resisting the flow of changes you are powerless to prevent.

Reversed:
It's time to grab those bootstraps and pull yourself back up. Whatever doesn't kill you makes you stronger and you're not dead.

Position 6—The Future

Upright:
The path you are on leads only to a dead end. There are no last-minute roads that will open up for you.

Reversed:
Try to make the best of a bad situation. Surely there is something good to come out of it?

Position 7—The Self

Upright:
The anguish you feel will eventually pass. Grieve as you must, but don't let it consume you.

Reversed:
There's no shame in starting over, especially if you know what you did wrong the first time and don't repeat it.

Position 8 —Outside Influences

Upright:
There are enemies wherever you turn. No help for it; you've got to pick up and move on alone.

Reversed:
Accept that helping hand that is being offered. You can use all the friends you can get right now.

Position 9 —Hopes and Fears

Upright:
Don't throw yourself under the bus to become a martyr to the cause—all is already lost and your effort will be wasted.

Reversed:
If there are those you have wronged along the way, now would be a good time to ask their forgiveness.

Position 10 —The Outcome

Upright:
Epic FAIL—that noise you hear is the sound of inevitability. You cannot run from the pain, but how much you suffer is up to you.

Reversed:
Thnk of this as a clean slate—you may have suffered a terrible setback, but you will bounce back again.

The Ten of Swords

Wands

The Ace of Wands

Feel the fire, feed the passion—Wands are about both. Aces are beginnings, so if you were looking for a nudge to get you started, here it is. Seize the moment with both hands and hang on for dear life.

Meaning in a Nutshell:
Passion

Position 1—The Situation

Upright:
There's a spark of creativity that just roared to life. Passions are ignited. *Ooh*, can't you just feel the excitement building?

Reversed:
Ho-hum. You're about as unmotivated as it gets. Yes, there is stuff to be done and you'll get to it—eventually.

Position 2—The Crossing

Upright:
Confidence is the key word here and you've got it. Don't be afraid to be ambitious, aim high and go for it.

Reversed:
No one is going to listen to your grand ideas if you don't get off your butt and do something about them.

Position 3—The Base

Upright:
There are new challenges being presented to you. Don't be intimidated—you are more capable than you might think.

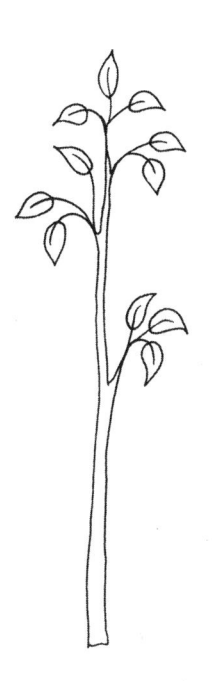

Reversed:
Don't get frustrated if it's not all falling into place like you'd hoped. Things just might need a bit more tweaking.

Position 4—The Past

Upright:
A flash of inspiration and suddenly the world as you knew it changed. Okay, maybe not quite that dramatic, but close.

Reversed:
In the NFL, a false start is just a penalty. Beginning before you're fully prepared is a recipe for disaster.

Position —The Crowning

Upright:
You're off to a great start—your future successes are being built on a sturdy foundation. Don't stop, keep going!

Reversed:
Overconfidence has been the ruin of many a rising star. Don't fall prey to the lure of lauding how great you are.

Position 6—The Future

Upright:
An attractive opportunity is going to present itself. There may be travel involved—give it some serious thought and consideration.

Reversed:
Things aren't off to the best start. Plans may be canceled, itineraries rearranged. The only constant is change—roll with it.

Position 7—The Self

Upright:
Idealistic with a fresh outlook, you are about as bright and fresh-faced as they get. Keep that energy level going.

Reversed:
C'mon, Eeyore—turn that frown upside down. Seriously, the pessimistic attitude not only holds you down, it holds you back.

Position 8 —Outside Influences

Upright:
Enthusiasm is contagious and you're a natural cheerleader. You'll get everyone around you fired up in a great way.

Reversed:
Not everyone is as enamored with your ideas as you. They'll try to shoot them full of holes out of spite.

Position 9 —Hopes and Fears

Upright:
Let your inner lion out. You've got all the courage you need to make your dreams into your reality.

Reversed:
Your impotence is apparent. Best put your plans on the back burner for now and go with what you know will work.

Position 10 —The Outcome

Upright:
You've got the desire and the drive. Now throw your initiative in gear and get busy working your magic.

Reversed:
You're not off to a good start. There is too much working against you and not much room for growth.

The Two of Wands

Waiting around is never fun, particularly if you're chomping at the bit to get things done. This Two is about maintaining a balance, so don't be in such a rush to arrive that you forget to enjoy the journey.

Meaning in a Nutshell:
Patience

Position 1—The Situation

Upright:
The cake is in the oven so find something productive to do while it bakes—it makes the wait time pass quicker.

Reversed:
You've got some real anxiety issues about the future. If you can't change it, don't freak out about it.

Position 2
—The Crossing

Upright:
Maybe two heads are better than one. Collaboration might be the way to go if you have the right partner.

Reversed:
You just can't seem to get into whatever is going on. Don't fake interest; that will backfire on you.

Position 3—The Base

Upright:
You need to take your responsibilities seriously. They are yours for a reason—only you can do it the way you do.

Reversed:
Even if others doubt your ability, don't allow them to shake your faith in yourself. You are stronger than you think.

Position 4—The Past

Upright:
You have (or had access to) amazing creative ability. Your vision for the future helped you lay a good foundation.

Reversed:
It's hard to fly with the eagles if your wings are constantly being clipped. Your fresh ideas aren't appreciated.

Position —The Crowning

Upright:
Now that you have an idea about why you're going, it's time to plan the wheres, whens, and hows.

Reversed:
Take a deep breath, count to ten—do whatever you have to regain control. Exercise a little patience, even if it kills you.

Position 6—The Future

Upright:
There are some negotiations coming up, so put your bargaining hat on. Don't be hasty in accepting the first offer.

Reversed:
When ambition is blind, it takes its toll on everyone around you. Be sensitive to the needs of others.

Position 7—The Self

Upright:
You're selling yourself a little short. You are capable of much more than you are admitting, especially to yourself.

Reversed:
Stop right there! Before you jump to the nearest conclusion, think long and hard. Things aren't always what they seem.

Position 8 —Outside Influences

Upright:
If you look, you'll find like-minded individuals itching to collaborate with you. Let them help you with fresh ideas.

Reversed:
Your loyalties are both misguided and misplaced. Someone is out to deceive you and, so far, their evil plan is working.

Position 9 —Hopes and Fears

Upright:
A little thinking outside the box would go a long way. Every problem has a solution if you look hard enough.

Reversed:
You're not facing reality—just because you don't want it to be isn't enough. Figure out how you're going to adjust.

Position 10 —The Outcome

Upright:
The time to make preparations for the future is now. Get your plan together and watch those pesky details.

Reversed:
Being cautious is okay, but being terrified to move for fear of a misstep isn't. Have faith in yourself.

The Three of Wands

It's payday. Time to reap some benefits from your hard work. You haven't quite arrived, but you've reached a "new to you" level of success. This Three delivers a congratulatory pat on the back, but don't stop working just yet.

Meaning in a Nutshell:
Rewards

Position 1—The Situation

Upright:
Your efforts are finally paying off and it's time to collect some accolades. Don't forget to smile and say thank you.

Reversed:
Not so fast there—there is still work left to do before you can color it done. You're rushing things.

Position 2
—The Crossing

Upright:
New opportunities are on the horizon and you're in the right position to capture them. Get that lasso ready; you'll need it.

Reversed:
A chance to change your future may have appeared but you were too busy to notice. Pay closer attention next time.

Position 3—The Base

Upright:
Your ship is heading into harbor now, so meet it with open arms. This is what you've been working towards.

Reversed:
Be confident, but don't underestimate the challenges that lie ahead—they'll bite you if you're not ready for them.

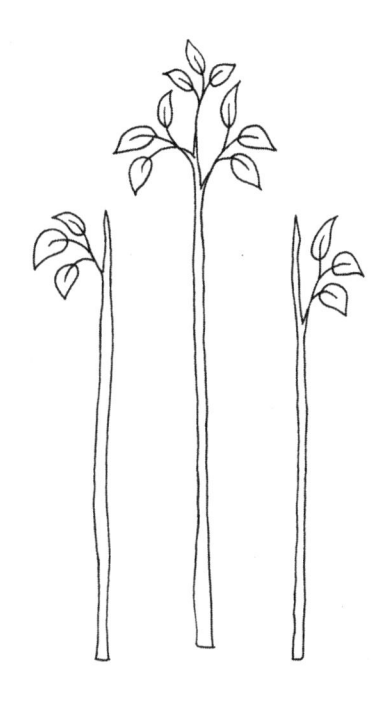

Position 4—The Past

Upright:
You were given some good advice and fortunately paid attention. Fortune favors the bold—you're living proof of the old adage.

Reversed:
Your miscalculations have landed you in hot water more than once. More homework and less assumption would have helped.

The Three of Wands

Position
—The Crowning

Upright:
It's a great day to be you, taking your success to the next level and shifting your energy into a higher gear.

Reversed:
No one minds you tooting your own horn, but don't blast them. Temper your arrogance with a dose of humility.

Position 6—The Future

Upright:
You've reached the next plateau; it's time to set a new goal—another rung in your ladder of success.

Reversed:
You need a new direction and fast. What you're doing isn't working—a classic case of right place/wrong time.

Position 7—The Self

Upright:
Your integrity won't let you stoop to underhanded tactics. Your ethics are admirable; you are setting a good example.

Reversed:
You're going to have to trust someone at some point. Get your due diligence in so that it isn't misplaced.

Position 8
—Outside Influences

Upright:
Your future success lies with a cooperative effort. Don't refuse the assistance of those wanting to help you do well.

Reversed:
Your smug attitude will only inspire others to jealousy of your good fortune. They'd love to see that look leave your face.

Position 9
—Hopes and Fears

Upright:
Dig out the old crystal ball—it's time to look into the future and get some Plan B ideas just in case.

Reversed:
It if can be expressed, it can be misunderstood. Choose your words carefully so that their meaning is absolutely clear.

Position 10
—The Outcome

Upright:
You've hit a level of success, but you're capable of more. Don't stop now; you're on a roll. Keep going!

Reversed:
Your aspirations are lofty, but your goals are not attainable at this time. Lower your expectations a little and try again.

The Four of Wands

One of the two cards that traditionally has no reversed meaning, the festive Four announces there is just cause to get your party on. Fun and good times abound. Reversed, you're just taking the scenic route to get there.

Meaning in a Nutshell:
Celebration

Position 1—The Situation

Upright:
Good times are coming, so get ready to put on the party hat and dancing shoes. It's time to relax, take a break and enjoy your current successes.

Reversed:
Even the brightest stars suffer a little burnout occasionally. Maybe a quiet evening in would be more to your liking.

Position 2—The Crossing

Upright:
A celebration is at hand, possibly for a marriage, birth, or other new beginning. There may be a change of residence.

Reversed:
Everyone has social anxiety at some point. Don't succumb to it, there's too much fun out there waiting to be had.

Position 3—The Base

Upright:
It's a great feeling knowing that you're the one in charge of your life. Survey your domain—it's good to be you.

Reversed:
You could be a little more grateful for the many blessings in your life. Don't take so much for granted.

Position 4—The Past

Upright:
Rest and relaxation is necessary to recharge your inner batteries. There's no reason to feel guilty about taking some.

Reversed:
No stranger to disappointment, you've had your share. Next time, make your desires known beforehand, so there's no room for misinterpretation.

Position —The Crowning

Upright:
Joy and happiness are yours—now would be a great time for a vacation to enjoy this feeling of peaceful satisfaction.

Reversed:
Time to rein it in a little; you're in danger of overdoing it. Guard against the "morning after" regrets.

Position 6—The Future

Upright:
You might not be looking to "git hitched," but you're ready to move on to the next square in your relationship.

Reversed:
A long term partnership may be coming to an end. Don't force it if it wasn't meant to be.

Position 7—The Self

Upright:
You're right to feel confident in your abilities—you are at the top of your game. Enjoy the freedom that competence brings.

Reversed:
There are unexpected obstacles popping up left and right. Don't let them throw off your groove, you're better than that.

Position 8 —Outside Influences

Upright:
There's no better time to get together with family and friends. Let them share the good times with you.

Reversed:
Don't give others the impression you're a snob. Let your hair down and encourage others to do the same.

Position 9 —Hopes and Fears

Upright:
In your dream, all the pieces are falling happily into place. Now work towards making it a waking reality.

Reversed:
A relationship is tolerated but unwanted. Who does it serve to prolong this one sided situation—you or them?

Position 10 —The Outcome

Upright:
You've reached the next level of success and should be proud of your achievement. Congratulations are in order!

Reversed:
There's still happiness ahead, but it's just going to take longer to get there. You'll catch up with the party later.

The Five of Wands

This Five heralds change in the form of competition. Get ready to put your game face on—there are challenges ahead and the playing field may or not be level. It's every man (or woman) for themselves, winner take all.

Meaning in a Nutshell:
Conflict

Position 1—The Situation

Upright:
The opposition has taken the field. Don't be afraid—those who fear challenge are usually unprepared for it anyway.

Reversed:
This isn't just a game. The other players have malicious intent at heart and the only rules are no rules.

Position 2

—The Crossing

Upright:
You've got some stiff competition ahead and the stakes are high. Bring your A-game or stay home.

Reversed:
You are being manipulated for someone else's gain, so be on guard if you didn't apply for the puppet position.

Position 3—The Base

Upright:
Twice the pride, double the fall—don't think yourself invincible; you'll get your butt handed to you every time.

Reversed:
There are some real communication problems complicating matters. Frustration has caused simple disagreements to blow up into outright hostility.

Position 4—The Past

Upright:
If you helped yourself to the lion's share before dividing the spoils, make sure you earned them first.

Reversed:
If you didn't observe the same rules as the other players—regardless of the reason why—you took unfair advantage.

Position
—The Crowning

Upright:
Don't fall into the "winning isn't everything; it's the only thing" trap. Keep your thoughts and actions in perspective.

Reversed:
Just because the others are playing dirty doesn't mean you have to. Don't be pulled down to their level.

Position 6—The Future

Upright:
You could be coerced or even forced into a compromise that you aren't very keen for. Watch for hidden loopholes.

Reversed:
Keep everything above board and don't leave anything to conjecture. Don't hand anyone the tools necessary to build your trap.

Position 7—The Self

Upright:
Your biggest battles are within yourself and inner conflict is tearing you apart. Pick an opinion and stay there.

Reversed:
Don't let petty grievances eat you alive. Nobody owes you anything and sore losers are no one's friend.

Position 8
—Outside Influences

Upright:
There is rivalry aplenty, but you can handle it. Nothing like a good, healthy competition to up your skill levels.

Reversed:
All the players may not have shown their faces yet. Don't rule out the possibility of hidden enemies.

Position 9
—Hopes and Fears

Upright:
It's the moment you've been waiting for—take the game to them instead of the other way around.

Reversed:
No way around it and no crying foul—the playing field isn't level. Adjust and do the best you can anyway.

Position 10
—The Outcome

Upright:
Yours isn't going to be an easy path; you'll be fighting every step of the way. Better pack a lunch.

Reversed:
Yours is a losing battle and you're wasting good energy better reapplied to more fruitful endeavors. Better luck next time.

The Six of Wands

All hail the conquering hero, returning to bask in the glory of the fans. This Six marks the end of a journey. As you make your acceptance speech, remember to thank all the people who helped you along the way.

Meaning in a Nutshell:
Pride

Position 1—The Situation

Upright:
You should be proud of your accomplishments. Know that you are indeed "all that and a bag of chips."

Reversed:
You are not using your power and authority for the high good of all concerned, and it is not going unnoticed.

Position 2—The Crossing

Upright:
There is some anticipated good news coming. Expect changes for the better as a result. Doors will be opened for you.

Reversed:
Ambition is healthy, but it's never a good idea to crush the dreams of others underfoot on your way up.

Position 3—The Base

Upright:
You're reached a sought-for goal. It wasn't easy—you've worked hard to be where you are. Enjoy the view!

Reversed:
Don't let stubborn pride prevent you from admitting you are wrong. Nobody's perfect. Everyone makes mistakes—even you.

Position 4—The Past

Upright:
Your accomplishments speak for themselves, but don't rely on past successes. What can you say you've done lately?

Reversed:
Feelings of inadequacy run deep, but you are your own worst critic. No one sees your faults as keenly as you.

Position
—The Crowning

Upright:
If you are waist deep in alligators and other people's drama, look for a resolution soon. Better times, they are a'coming.

Reversed:
Don't let yourself be used to bring glory and recognition to those who earned it by exploiting others.

Position 6—The Future

Upright:
It may be to your advantage to consider the current offer. It might open up a whole new world for you.

Reversed:
Not putting forth enough effort has left you lost in the crowd. You could've been a contender had you tried harder.

Position 7—The Self

Upright:
For the moment, you're satisfied and content with the status quo. Enjoy it; you'll be ready for the next challenge soon enough.

Reversed:
Envy isn't one of the seven deadly sins for nothing—it will eat you alive if you let it.

Position 8
—Outside Influences

Upright:
You'll be welcomed into your circle with open arms. You've been gifted with a great bunch of supporters.

Reversed:
Frenemies (enemies pretending to be friends) are something you don't need. Watch for smiles that don't quite meet the eyes.

Position 9
—Hopes and Fears

Upright:
You know you want the buzz that the power brings. You're looking for admiration or validation from others.

Reversed:
A little self esteem, liberally applied, would do you good. Stop worrying that you won't be up to the challenge.

Position 10
—The Outcome

Upright:
You have arrived. Give credit where it is due and thank all the little people who helped you get there.

Reversed:
You have snatched defeat from the jaws of victory rather than the other way around. Better luck next time.

The Seven of Wands

The crowd turned fickle and you've found yourself defending the higher ground, either literally or figuratively. Either way, you're on your own, but you can handle it. The Seven encourages you to draw your power from within, not without.

Meaning in a Nutshell:
Resolve

Position 1—The Situation

Upright:
Don't let them back you into a corner—stand your ground in your own defense. You can do this!

Reversed:
You are right to feel threatened. This time, it's not just your imagination acting up. Prepare for battle.

Position 2—The Crossing

Upright:
Your inner strength and resolve are going to be tested. Don't react without thinking through the ramifications first.

Reversed:
Playing the victim doesn't serve anyone, least of all you. Don't give up your power without a struggle.

Position 3—The Base

Upright:
You have the courage of your convictions behind you. You know that the cause you fight for is a worthy one.

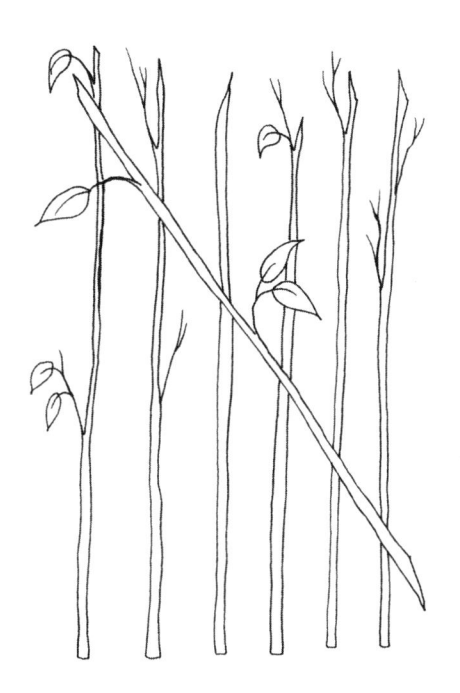

Reversed:
Running from your problems is the coward's way out. They don't go away—avoidance only extends the pain and anxiety.

Position 4—The Past

Upright:
Your willingness to stand up for what you believe in has established your reputation as a fair and honorable person.

Reversed:
Everyone gets rejected as some point. You just took yours a little harder than most. Fine—now get past it.

Position
—The Crowning

Upright:
You've got some challenges ahead. Find the middle ground between overconfident and freaked out to dig your toes in.

Reversed:
Sitting on the fence gets you nothing but splinters in the butt. Deliberate, pick a side, and commit to the outcome.

Position 6—The Future

Upright:
There is an opportunity to advance your cause. Gain leverage by doing your homework before it is required of you.

Reversed:
Those who fight and run away live to fight another day. There's no shame in retreat if done honorably.

Position 7—The Self

Upright:
You've got amazing levels of emotional and mental strength when facing adversity. You are stronger than you think.

Reversed:
Calling yourself a failure is a self-fulfilling prophecy. Try to focus on your good points and quit being so negative.

Position 8
—Outside Influences

Upright:
Full steam ahead—your friends and allies have your back. Feel secure in the knowledge that you won't be alone.

Reversed:
Extremism takes many forms and guises to fool you. Don't be fooled by pretty lies and empty gestures of goodwill.

Position 9
—Hopes and Fears

Upright:
This is a great opportunity to show what you're made of. Seize the moment and make the competition sweat.

Reversed:
Behind-the-scenes activity is putting you at a disadvantage. You may wish to postpone your plans for your debut.

Position 10
—The Outcome

Upright:
It's time to put your money where your mouth is—you're about to be tested. Hold fast and you will persevere.

Reversed:
If you are overcompensating for something, it won't be a secret. Don't get everyone's attention until you know you're ready.

The Eight of Wands

Think fast—something's coming your way. It might be a message, maybe an opportunity. Either way, get ready to act when it arrives—this Eight encourages you to prepare now so that you won't waffle when the time comes.

Meaning in a Nutshell:
Urgency

Position 1—The Situation

Upright:
You've got something coming your way fast. Some call this the "falling in love" card. Whatever you call it, brace yourself.

Reversed:
Hurry up and wait—you've reached a standstill. All of your forward progress has rolled to a screeching halt.

Position 2—The Crossing

Upright:
Can't you feel the excitement in the air? It's building all around you, waiting for something epic to happen.

Reversed:
You are expending a lot of energy imagining the worst possible outcomes. If you can't fix it, don't fret about it.

Position 3—The Base

Upright:
The goal is within reach. Great form, but you better get busier than just posing if you want to reap the rewards of your efforts.

Reversed:
You've got too much going on to think straight. Clear out your schedule and social calendar; delegate busywork to others.

Position 4—The Past

Upright:
Things have happened quickly for you, but you were able to rise to the occasion. Stay flexible and open.

Reversed:
Everywhere you turned someone was trying to throw a wrench into the process. It taught you to expect the unexpected, though.

Position
—The Crowning

Upright:
Events have been set in motion that cannot be called back. Strap yourself in and prepare for a wild ride.

Reversed:
Cutting corners and taking shortcuts is no way to get ahead and stay ahead. All your efforts have been wasted.

Position 6—The Future

Upright:
There may be travel ahead, so be ready to make lightning fast decisions. You may receive an apology soon.

Reversed:
No doubt about it—you underestimated your competition and got caught with your pants down. Go nap on your own time!

Position 7—The Self

Upright:
You've got the fires of your creativity banked. Take the initiative to let it out and see what lights up.

Reversed:
You need to get both your mouth and your emotions back under control fast. If you owe someone an apology, get busy.

Position 8
—Outside Influences

Upright:
Things couldn't be any better if you had planned it all out. It's all coming together, just like you wanted.

Reversed:
Don't be jealous of what everyone else has—get out there and get it for yourself. Be proactive.

Position 9
—Hopes and Fears

Upright:
You have drawn the bow and let your arrow fly. If your planning was complete, it will find its target.

Reversed:
Don't grip the reins so tightly, allow for some spontaneity in your life. Lighten up—you never know what will happen.

Position 10
—The Outcome

Upright:
Look for important communications. A "like" affair could be turning into love— you'll just have to watch for the signs.

Reversed:
Don't be waiting at the airport when your ship comes in. Slow down and listen more carefully to what you're being told.

The Nine of Wands

Ever on guard, nothing is going to slip past you — or is it? The Nine doesn't want you to slide into paranoia, but advises you stay alert for suspicious goings on. Don't let trouble catch you napping on your watch.

Meaning in a Nutshell:
Vigilance

Position 1—The Situation

Upright:
Stay alert and on guard. There could be trouble ahead — be ready to nip it in the bud.

Reversed:
Anything can and will get by you if you're not paying attention. Now isn't the time to let your mind wander.

Position 2 —The Crossing

Upright:
Listen closely to what's being said, closer to what isn't. Miscommunications can start wars if you're not careful.

Reversed:
Putting up barriers is a good idea if you've already got everything you need — not so much, if you don't.

Position 3—The Base

Upright:
Defensive maneuvers: now is the time for fortification. Watch details and make sure everyone's story is on the same page.

Reversed:
Predators take advantage of those they can separate from the herd. Don't be a part of their food chain.

Position 4—The Past

Upright:
You pay attention by keeping your eyes/ears open and your mouth closed — isn't it amazing what you learn that way?

Reversed:
Now you're ready. No, NOW you're ready. It sucks being caught off guard, especially if you can't get a do-over.

Position —The Crowning

Upright:
Now isn't the time to make any large decisions. Adopt a wait-and-see attitude until you have all the necessary information.

Reversed:
When it comes to initiative, you're about a quart low. Try to remember why you want what you want.

Position 6—The Future

Upright:
Obstacles are popping up left and right, some expected, some not. Don't let the surprises break your stride.

Reversed:
You might as well stop chafing against the bit, trying to force change. Delays are a fact of life.

Position 7—The Self

Upright:
You are the very soul of resilience. Stay flexible and you won't get bent out of shape by minor frustrations.

Reversed:
Are you refusing to budge because it really isn't a good idea or is it because you're too stubborn to move?

Position 8 —Outside Influences

Upright:
You're fortunate to have stability in your current environment. Delegate responsibility; don't take it all on yourself.

Reversed:
Not everyone has your best interests at heart, no matter how noble their words or well meaning their intentions.

Position 9 —Hopes and Fears

Upright:
Take care of yourself, watch for stress-related health problems. Practice learning how to still the mind and relax.

Reversed:
This is the "naked at the grocery store" dream. Get your stuff together now so that you're not caught unprepared.

Position 10 —The Outcome

Upright:
You have challenges coming. If you keep your chin up and your head held high, you will win the day.

Reversed:
You're turning molehills into mountains, convinced everyone is out to get you. Maybe so, maybe no. Either way — chill out.

The Ten of Wands

You're lugging the weight of the world on your shoulders. Insisting on carrying your burdens alone isn't doing your back, your mind, or your social calendar any good. Ten is the end of the cycle—time to lighten your load.

Meaning in a Nutshell:
Burdens

Position 1—The Situation

Upright:
You've got more burdens than the law allows. Everybody and their brother is using you as an emotional pack mule.

Reversed:
Heave a sigh of relief as your burden eases. You might not be rid of it yet, but it's a start.

Position 2—The Crossing

Upright:
Your obligations are weighing heavily upon you. It's a big responsibility, knowing how much is expected from you.

Reversed:
Realize that you can't do it all alone. There's no shame in asking for—and accepting—help from others.

Position 3—The Base

Upright:
You're in danger of becoming a workaholic with no life at all. Those who care about you miss you.

Reversed:
It's okay to have a little fun to recharge your batteries, but don't shirk your responsibilities to do it.

Position 4—The Past

Upright:
Stress has run you into the ground. Your prior obligations became too much for you to comfortably handle.

Reversed:
You didn't volunteer for your workload—more likely it was dumped on you without your consent, creating resentment.

Position —The Crowning

Upright:
You've got too many things drawing on your time and energy, but it's not getting any better right now.

Reversed:
Look to catch a much-needed break. Be ready to take full advantage of it and enjoy it while it lasts.

Position 6—The Future

Upright:
You're taking on more than you can conceivably do, setting you up to fail on an epic level.

Reversed:
Worrying about a thing is often worse than the thing itself. Let go of anxiety before it affects your health.

Position 7—The Self

Upright:
Martyrdom is a lonely place to be. No one ever appreciates your sacrifices as much as you do.

Reversed:
You hoped things would get better and they did, but not as much as you were expecting. Color you under-whelmed.

Position 8 —Outside Influences

Upright:
A lot of people depend on you and you are finding you don't like being indispensable. Delegate some of your authority.

Reversed:
There are plenty of loving hands available. Accept their nurturing; they want to help you lighten your load.

Position 9 —Hopes and Fears

Upright:
No end in sight—the oppression will continue, even if morale improves. Take comfort in the fact that nothing lasts forever.

Reversed:
Be careful or you'll be the one left holding the bag. Don't accept the blame if you're not at fault.

Position 10 —The Outcome

Upright:
You are overextending, isolating yourself from life and love. Is being successful an adequate trade for your happiness?

Reversed:
You are capable of overcoming the limitations put on you. Do what you can, release what you can't.

Cups

The Ace of Cups

Aces are beginnings, Cups are Emotions — Love is in the air for sure. When you see this card, look for matters of the heart to be at the heart of the matter. Remember, there are all kinds of partnerships.

Meaning in a Nutshell:
Infatuation

Position 1—The Situation

Upright:
If you can't eat, sleep, or think straight, it must be new love. Enjoy the tsunami of delicious feelings.

Reversed:
Nothing is rousing your passions these days. You are very detached and unemotional, almost as if you were asleep.

Position 2 —The Crossing

Upright:
You could be receiving an invitation soon. Accept it with a smile — you never know what great things could happen.

Reversed:
The object of your affection doesn't feel the same way. It's hard to be in a relationship when only one cares.

Position 3—The Base

Upright:
Your intuition is blossoming into awareness. This is one time when you should trust your heart over your head.

Reversed:
You are mired in a pit of stagnation, not moving forward and not moving back. You need help getting unstuck.

Position 4—The Past

Upright:
You made a real breakthrough, reconciling personal desires with intellectual needs. There really is a comfortable median between the two.

Reversed:
Someone has been toying with someone else's emotions. That's never nice, even if they DO deserve it.

Position
—The Crowning

Upright:
There is an emotional beginning ahead, one that you feel good about and are looking forward to. Could this be love?

Reversed:
Don't start picking out your china pattern just yet. This relationship will be short lived, so enjoy it while it lasts.

Position 6—The Future

Upright:
A breath of fresh air is going to blow through your relationship, making it feel shiny and new all over again.

Reversed:
The new relationship, although off to a promising start, isn't as invigorating as you had hoped. Try not to yawn.

Position 7—The Self

Upright:
Don't you love to be in love? Colors are brighter and life is sweet. Capture this feeling and keep it close.

Reversed:
Someone could do with more understanding and less ego. Don't be so quick to judge that you miss all the facts.

Position 8
—Outside Influences

Upright:
You're surrounded by people who are filled with peace and contentment. Everyone is so happy for you.

Reversed:
The absence of love isn't hate—it is apathy. It is possible to be lonely, even if you're surrounded by people.

Position 9
—Hopes and Fears

Upright:
It is your desire to form a lasting relationship. You can start by making yourself as lovable as possible.

Reversed:
Better take off those rose-colored glasses—you're being led on. Make sure your partner feels the same as you.

Position 10
—The Outcome

Upright:
Oh, Joy! Oh, Rapture! Yes, love is a many splendored thing. Enjoy this special time for the wonder that it is.

Reversed:
Insecurity can be a real problem, especially if it keeps you from enjoying a relationship you desperately want.

The Ace of Cups

The Two of Cups

The Two halves are becoming a whole. The new partnership might be thinking of taking it to a more permanent level. Make sure it is your head and heart together that makes the final decision. Cooperative efforts are the key.

**Meaning in a Nutshell:
Partnership**

Position 1—The Situation

Upright:
Get ready to pair off! Partnerships are favored. There could be a marriage or other long-term form of commitment.

Reversed:
Someone is coming down with a bad case of disillusionment and the whole situation is heading for heartache fast.

Position 2—The Crossing

Upright:
There's a bad case of attraction in the air. Better look and see who is doing the checking out.

Reversed:
They say that forbidden fruit is the sweetest. Just remember what happens if you're caught sampling a bite...or two.

Position 3—The Base

Upright:
A match made in heaven? Maybe—it's time to discover if you two really are meant for each other.

Reversed:
What started out strong has weakened and is in danger of breaking altogether. This partnership is sinking fast.

Position 4—The Past

Upright:
Mutual trust has sent up a good, solid foundation for the future, provided it is kept up and nurtured.

Reversed:
This relationship has been a roller coaster ride, a series of ups and downs and not much in between.

Position
—The Crowning

Upright:
What you get is what you give. Appreciate the ones you love and know that it will be returned to you.

Reversed:
The air is full of destructive words and emotions. It might be time to step back and distance yourself from the drama.

Position 6—The Future

Upright:
You're in for a pleasant surprise—someone you may think hasn't noticed you has, and in a big kinda way.

Reversed:
Don't be fooled into believing pretty words that have no basis in reality—it's the actions that really count.

Position 7—The Self

Upright:
When you wear your heart upon your sleeve, your love cannot doubt your sincerity. Be careful who else sees it, though.

Reversed:
Jealousy will end up driving the one you seek so desperately to hold away. Rein it in or at least disguise it.

Position 8
—Outside Influences

Upright:
Let those around you know you are in it with them all the way. Empathize with their pain, share in their happiness.

Reversed:
You don't always have to be the star. Being overly possessive and demanding will leave you feeling alone and isolated.

Position 9
—Hopes and Fears

Upright:
Find a common ground between you and the object of your desire. The more interests you share, the closer you'll become.

Reversed:
Beware of promises made in the heat of passion. They have a tendency to cool off the next morning.

Position 10
—The Outcome

Upright:
A sought-after commitment might be at hand. If the love is strong enough, together you can make it work.

Reversed:
A major shift of priorities is needed but one or both parties aren't willing to go to the trouble.

The Two of Cups

The Three of Cups

Girls Night Out—time to celebrate the sisterhood with like-minded individuals. This Three reminds us that Love binds us to each other, regardless of the circumstance of birth. Your family is who you care about and who cares about you.

**Meaning in a Nutshell:
Jubilation**

Position 1—The Situation

Upright:
Prepare for a party—whether there is something to celebrate or not, get together with good friends and enjoy yourself.

Reversed:
Everything has slid to a firm and grinding halt. All good things must come to an end sometime.

Position 2

—The Crossing

Upright:
Happy anticipation is the best, most satisfying kind—something good is coming your way and you can hardly wait.

Reversed:
Back off a bit and settle down. Overdoing it early is a good way to miss out on all the fun later.

Position 3—The Base

Upright:
There could be an engagement to announce, a birth, or marriage. Creatively speaking, the sky is the limit.

Reversed:
A situation draws to a close and not a moment too soon. Let go and let the healing process begin.

Position 4—The Past

Upright:
A long-awaited reunion has put you on your current path. Figure out what separated you and don't repeat past mistakes.

Reversed:
No one has ever died from embarrassment, but that's not to say people haven't wanted to. It happened—forget it.

Position

—The Crowning

Upright:
If you are a gambling person, look for a favorable outcome to your most recent risk. Expect rampant happiness.

Reversed:
There is no "clear history" button on your sex life. Tone it down before your reputation begins to precede you.

Position 6—The Future

Upright:
You're been working hard; you've earned some quality chill time for yourself. Take it with no guilt whatsoever.

Reversed:
Personal addictions can take many forms, some pretty, others not so much. Balance your needs against your got-to-haves.

Position 7—The Self

Upright:
Adrift in a sea of contentment, all is well in your world. You feel complete and fulfilled for a change.

Reversed:
Remember what you were and what you are, but don't forget what you're going to be. Stop living in the past.

Position 8

—Outside Influences

Upright:
You have a strong community of friends and family surrounding you. Your strengths complement each other. Draw on their experience.

Reversed:
Even the most idle gossip has the ability to do irreparable damage. Take care in what you repeat.

Position 9

—Hopes and Fears

Upright:
All bright-eyed and bushy-tailed: it's okay to be exuberant, but don't burn all your energy at once. Pace yourself.

Reversed:
Major change of plans—don't get bent out of shape; there isn't anything you can do about it anyway.

Position 10

—The Outcome

Upright:
Rejoice in that you are loved with those who love you. Everything else is just icing on the cake.

Reversed:
Don't stay so focused on the sky that you miss the ground cracking beneath your feet. The situation is unstable.

The Four of Cups

Too much of a good thing is not a good thing. Fours suggest rest and reflection—in the Cups, we are reminded to count our blessings and be grateful for what we have. Lose the spoiled and pampered sense of entitlement.

Meaning in a Nutshell:
Apathy

Position 1—The Situation

Upright:
You're extremely dissatisfied with the current situation, even if you can't quite put your finger on what's wrong.

Reversed:
Shake off those doldrums— you've got a burst of new energy just raring to go. Time to get up and get busy.

Position 2—The Crossing

Upright:
Don't allow yourself to become so jaded that you can no longer find joy in the simple pleasures of life. Slow down, don't move so fast.

Reversed:
Change is afoot and not a moment too soon. At this point, you'd be happy with almost anything different.

Position 3—The Base

Upright:
A lot of activities sound good when you're bored. Don't let having nothing to do lead you to doing the wrong things.

Reversed:
Careful, your shallowness is showing. Reconsider your current behavior and try making it a little less about you.

Position 4—The Past

Upright:
You haven't been the most stable lover, at times bordering on fickle and flighty. Work on sticking around longer.

Reversed:
When you got tired of waiting around for things to happen, you got up and did it yourself. Good initiative!

Position 5—The Crowning

Upright:
No matter what you say or do, you can't seem to fill that emptiness inside. Nothing satisfies your needs.

Reversed:
With a fresh new outlook, you're starting to see things with a less than jaundiced eye. Perk up and smile!

Position 6—The Future

Upright:
You've got the whole inner turmoil thing down to an art form. Narrow down the pros and cons, then pick a side.

Reversed:
A little bit of self-esteem will take you a long way. Stop being so critical, holding yourself to unattainable standards.

Position 7—The Self

Upright:
Like attracts like, so if you are putting out negative "poor me" vibes, you will get more in return.

Reversed:
In dreams come the answers to your unspoken questions. Pay attention to yours; write them down for later.

Position 8—Outside Influences

Upright:
If you feel put upon and obligated just to be nice, it's a safe assumption you'd rather be somewhere else.

Reversed:
If you don't even try to help yourself out of your mistakes, don't expect others to come rushing in to save you from yourself.

Position 9—Hopes and Fears

Upright:
You're suffering from the depressing feeling that this is as good as it gets. Remember that low morale is contagious.

Reversed:
Now would be a great time to break the worry chain and start using your time and energy more effectively.

Position 10—The Outcome

Upright:
Your own lack of initiative is causing your inertia. Don't let apathy make you lose sight of what's important to you.

Reversed:
Amazing new opportunities will be opening to you. Get a new lease on life and prepare to get busy.

The Five of Cups

Fives indicate change which can be painful if we allow it. This Five is so busy looking at what has been lost that it is blinded to what still remains. Take time to grieve and heal, but don't forget to move forward.

Meaning in a Nutshell:
Regret

Position 1—The Situation

Upright:
You're so busy missing what you've lost that you're losing sight of what you still have. Show a little gratitude.

Reversed:
Yes, it hurt but you've learned from the pain. Moving on is the best way of putting the past behind you.

Position 2

—The Crossing

Upright:
There is a certain comfort in routine. You have always gravitated towards the familiar, rather than trying something new.

Reversed:
The bandage hurts more when you pull it off slowly, so just yank it off. Fear faced is fear displaced.

Reversed:
Confronting your shortcomings head on is the only way. Take a hard look in the mirror, then fix what's wrong.

Position 3—The Base

Upright:
Drowning in self-pity is a slow, numbing death. It's also a real buzz kill for those around you. Cheer up.

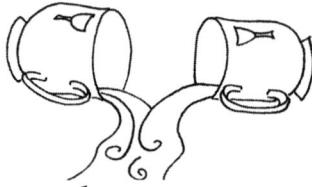

Position 4—The Past

Upright:
Betrayal is a part of life, albeit a very painful part. Carrying around a grudge is no way to get your exercise.

Reversed:
The best thing about making mistakes is all the experience you get by learning from them. You did learn, right?

Position
—The Crowning

Upright:
The path you're on won't benefit you in the long run, but it's you who needs to step up and realize that.

Reversed:
It's time to turn over a new leaf and leave the past behind. You're getting that coveted second chance.

Position 6—The Future

Upright:
The answer is there, right in front of your eyes. If you choose not to see it, it changes nothing.

Reversed:
Someone from your past could be returning for purposes unknown. Better get Plans A, B, and C ready, just in case.

Position 7—The Self

Upright:
Nobody likes a Drama Queen/King—they are exhausting to be around. Focus on something besides your own troubles.

Reversed:
You've got reason to be optimistic. Everyone who has tried to drag you down has failed—you're stronger than they thought.

Position 8
—Outside Influences

Upright:
Isolating yourself away from family and friends is not a good idea. You need nurturing human contact right now.

Reversed:
Be grateful for your friends—they are supportive and would go to any length to help if you would allow it.

Position 9
—Hopes and Fears

Upright:
A serious re-evaluation of priorities is in order. In other words, You, reality. Reality, you. Nice for the two of you to meet.

Reversed:
It may seem dark out now, but the sun really will come out again—just like in the song.

Position 10
—The Outcome

Upright:
Regret is a silent killer of the soul. The past won't change, so don't waste precious time lamenting what could have been.

Reversed:
Your happiness and joy will soon return—today is the first day of your new beginning. Make this one count.

The Five of Cups

The Six of Cups

It's always fun to revisit fond childhood memories. The Six brings harmony through past experiences. Draw strength from them and enjoy, but try not to dwell on what was—the past is great to visit, but don't build a house there.

**Meaning in a Nutshell:
Nostalgia**

Position 1—The Situation

Upright:
Look for a blast from the past—perhaps the return of an old friend/lover or just a reminder of good times.

Reversed:
Brushing away the cobwebs of yesterday, you're ready for a new challenge moving forward into the future.

Position 2—The Crossing

Upright:
There could be a reunion of old friends. Get ready to share some of those memorable "back in the day" stories.

Reversed:
Your past is coming back to haunt you. When confronted with it, remember to think, then act, not the other way around.

Position 3—The Base

Upright:
There may be a Karmic lesson for you in the current situation. What about all this seems familiar to you?

Reversed:
Just because you refuse to grow up doesn't mean the world will adjust itself to suit you. Stop being childish.

Position 4—The Past

Upright:
Everything was bigger, brighter, and faster back in the day. Make sure your memories aren't tarnished by selectivity.

Reversed:
Everyone has moments they'd rather not remember. You put yours behind you and created a new future for yourself.

Position
—The Crowning

Upright:
There could be a change in job or possible travel in your future, should you accept the offered opportunity.

Reversed:
You're dragging around way too much emotional baggage. It's time to forgive both yourself and others to lighten the load.

Position 6—The Future

Upright:
You are in line for a family inheritance—maybe dishes or a family secret recipe. Be grateful for the gift.

Reversed:
Nothing like a monkey wrench in the plans to put everyone's teeth on edge—plan on postponements and delays.

Position 7—The Self

Upright:
You are riddled with indecision. Make a list of the pros and cons if you must, but you need to choose.

Reversed:
Nothing is perfect all the time. Disappointments happen to the best of us. Breathe deeply. This too will pass.

Position 8
—Outside Influences

Upright:
Look for good times with good friends, catching up all the latest and recounting all the greatest. Have fun!

Reversed:
Everyone has a skeleton—or three—in the old family closet. Not all secrets should be shared, though.

Position 9
—Hopes and Fears

Upright:
If you wanted to reunite with someone in your past, now may be the time. Don't wait for an excuse.

Reversed:
You've made poor choices in the past and are in danger of making another now. Reconsider before it's too late.

Position 10
—The Outcome

Upright:
Enjoy your walk down memory lane, but keep in mind that you're just revisiting, not moving in.

Reversed:
Given your current state of arrested development, try to do the mature thing, even if it's not much fun.

The Seven of Cups

Choices, choices—with so many tempting options, what's one to do? The Seven invites you to take the debate inside to sort out what you really want. Daydreams are fun, but in the long run accomplish nothing if you don't act.

Meaning in a Nutshell:
Dreams

Position 1—The Situation

Upright:
Daydreaming is a lovely way to pass a few moments, but it is distracting when you're trying to get things done.

Reversed:
For the first time in a long time, you're seeing things for what they are. Change of opinion in 5, 4, 3…

Position 2—The Crossing

Upright:
It's good to have high aspirations, but they can quickly turn into unrealistic expectations if you're not careful.

Reversed:
Way to step up and take responsibility for your own actions! Kudos to you for acting with forethought and maturity.

Position 3—The Base

Upright:
This way, that way, the other way—there are too many choices at hand, too many hard decisions to be made.

Reversed:
Everything is better with a healthy dose of reality. Seeing clearly is the only way out of the current quagmire.

Position 4—The Past

Upright:
Escapism might have seemed like a good idea at the time, but it prevented you from getting anything done.

Reversed:
Although it was hard going for a while, give yourself credit for having plucked some good choices from the offered options.

Position

—The Crowning

Upright:
At life's buffet, you are boggled by the multitude of choices. Pick something and move on—you're holding up the line.

Reversed:
You've got the right stuff to get things done. Your drive and determination will serve you well.

Position 6—The Future

Upright:
Your friends won't continue putting up with your selfish indulgences. Try thinking of someone's needs other than your own.

Reversed:
Pay close attention to the seemingly insignificant details. Good follow through will make all the difference in the world.

Position 7—The Self

Upright:
There are appropriate means of escapism. Substance abuse is not acceptable. If it's that bad, talk to someone about it.

Reversed:
You've got your eyes on the prize. The current downtime is just so that you can fine tune your battle strategy.

Position 8

—Outside Influences

Upright:
You're getting lots of lip service. For right now, don't count on anyone to do what they say they will.

Reversed:
Just like dominoes, suddenly all the pieces are falling into place. It's great when it works like you planned it.

Position 9

—Hopes and Fears

Upright:
You have been gifted with a great imagination. Use it to open up even more options for your future.

Reversed:
You work hard but are secretly afraid of succeeding. Don't be so quick to declare yourself a failure.

Position 10

—The Outcome

Upright:
All the great plans in the world will come to nothing if all you do is daydream about them.

Reversed:
Your goals are attainable, now that you know which ones to pursue. Break time is over—get back to work.

The Eight of Cups

Sometimes even our best efforts aren't enough to turn the tide. There's no shame in realizing when a battle just isn't worth winning. The Eight brings a challenge to face the harsh truth and act accordingly, even when it hurts.

Meaning in a Nutshell:
Abandonment

Position 1—The Situation

Upright:
You've had a change of heart that has caused everything to come to a sliding halt. Think hard before proceeding.

Reversed:
Sometimes it is hard to let go, especially if you don't want to. Facing the truth can be hard.

Position 2 —The Crossing

Upright:
It's time to cut your losses, and step back to assess the situation and figure out where you screwed up.

Reversed:
If you are unwilling to change the way you do things, don't be surprised if nothing ever changes.

Position 3—The Base

Upright:
Knowing which battles to fight and which to walk away from is a valuable skill. Keep your options open.

Reversed:
You are throwing good energy after bad. All your time and effort is being wasted on your current venture.

Position 4—The Past

Upright:
All that glitters isn't gold and you just got your first glimpse of what lies beneath. It wasn't worth the effort.

Reversed:
Stubbornness and a refusal to change with the times made things stagnant. Learn from these past mistakes.

Position —The Crowning

Upright:
Someone has come down with a definite fear of emotional intimacy. Don't look for any type of commitment here.

Reversed:
Some things never change. No matter how good a game they talk, it's their actions you need to watch.

Position 6—The Future

Upright:
It is better to sever all ties and make a clean break than to keep hanging on in false hope.

Reversed:
Don't aspire to cut corners and just get by. You don't want to be the "me" in mediocrity.

Position 7—The Self

Upright:
You're right to feel a sense of discontent. Things haven't been going well for some time now. Trust your instincts.

Reversed:
Sticking your head in the sand like as ostrich accomplishes nothing. The situation won't get any better that way.

Position 8 —Outside Influences

Upright:
Pay attention—the emotional climate of your immediate friends is changing. It might be time to distance yourself.

Reversed:
You're stuck in a rut, doing the same things with the same people every single day. Shake it up a little.

Position 9 —Hopes and Fears

Upright:
Sometimes silence speaks much louder than words. Maybe it's time to go inside yourself for a while.

Reversed:
If you are so narrow-minded that you can only see your point of view, you'll never get the problems resolved.

Position 10 —The Outcome

Upright:
Sometimes you just gotta walk away with your head up and not look back. This is one of those times.

Reversed:
It's the same old situation—same thing, different day. Nothing is going to change unless you change it.

The Eight of Cups

The Nine of Cups

Congratulations! This is the Wish card, one of the happiest in Tarot. Don't be surprised if your wildest desires become your reality. Anything is possible if you believe, so be careful in what you wish for—you just might get it.

Meaning in a Nutshell:
Wishes

Position 1—The Situation

Upright:
All is well in your world—your needs are being met in a satisfactory way and you are content.

Reversed:
Don't let how good things are lull you into a sense of complacency. It's good right now, but be alert anyway.

Position 2—The Crossing

Upright:
Someone waved a magic wand and all your dreams are coming true. Don't look a gift horse in the mouth.

Reversed:
Don't let all the present goodness go to your head—there is a fine line between enjoyment and outright debauchery.

Position 3—The Base

Upright:
You are experiencing a sense of fulfillment you haven't known before. Relax and enjoy it while it lasts.

Reversed:
It is necessary to love yourself, but don't be so self-absorbed that you forget about the needs of others.

Position 4—The Past

Upright:
You've caught a number of lucky breaks. Being in the right place at the right time has helped you immensely.

Reversed:
There's a downside to having all your needs provided for: you didn't learn how to work for them.

Position
—The Crowning

Upright:
Happiness and joy abounds—it is a glorious time to be alive. Remember to be grateful for what you have.

Reversed:
The world is full of imperfections. If you nitpick and criticize everything you get, you'll never enjoy anything.

Position 6—The Future

Upright:
If you have a goal you've been working hard towards, look for good news and intense personal gratification soon.

Reversed:
You are in danger of letting greed override your good sense—you might want to see to that.

Position 7—The Self

Upright:
You've got a warm, fuzzy sense of security and satisfaction. Count your blessings and let yourself enjoy them.

Reversed:
Always looking for the next great and exciting thing, you're an adrenaline junkie. Why are you so bored?

Position 8
—Outside Influences

Upright:
You know that all you need to do is ask and you will receive. Be grateful for your loving support group.

Reversed:
Watch for rampant insincerity—those who are too quick to agree with you usually have a secondary agenda.

Position 9
—Hopes and Fears

Upright:
Situations can take strange twists and turns without any warning. Make sure you know exactly what you want.

Reversed:
Nobody owes you anything, so the better-than-you attitude can go away. Smugness isn't a pretty quality.

Position 10
—The Outcome

Upright:
If you have a wish, it could be coming true. Be appreciative and thank all those who made your happiness possible.

Reversed:
Careful what you wish for—you just might get it. It may not be as good as you thought it would be.

The Ten of Cups

Tens are the end of a cycle and this one is the culmination of a happy relationship—love, maybe partnership or some other form of commitment. Everyone's definition of Happily Ever After is different—results may vary; some assembly required.

Meaning in a Nutshell: Contentment

Position 1—The Situation

Upright:
Happiness and joy reign supreme. The sun rises on a beautiful day filled with butterflies and rainbows—yeah, it's like that.

Reversed:
There are few things worse that arguing with friends or family. Is the reason for disagreement that important?

Position 2—The Crossing

Upright:
Regardless of what minor difficulties are annoying you at the moment, rest assured that harmony will soon be restored.

Reversed:
Don't allow yourself to sink into depression. Let those who care about you know what troubles you.

Position 3—The Base

Upright:
Family doesn't have to be about who you're related to—it's about who you love and who loves you back.

Reversed:
A separation or distance could cause heartache. Try to heal the rift before it gets out of hand.

Position 4—The Past

Upright:
Blood is thicker than water— you're not above using that as your battle cry to get things done.

Reversed:
Before asking why your orders weren't carried out, perhaps you should question if your demands were reasonable.

Position
—The Crowning

Upright:
A cycle is coming to a close and all is in perfect harmony. This is the "lived happily ever after" part.

Reversed:
Be artsy or revolutionary if you want to, but no one is going to suffer your antisocial behavior for long.

Position 6—The Future

Upright:
This is the white house, picket fence, two kids, and a dog card — look for a happy resolution to your question.

Reversed:
Don't look for smooth sailing ahead — there is a big fly in the ointment, messing things up. Delays are likely.

Position 7—The Self

Upright:
Appreciate what you have and be generous with what you can. Learn the difference between sympathy and empathy.

Reversed:
No one is an island. Don't turn your back on your family unit just because you got a little scolding.

Position 8
—Outside Influences

Upright:
You have a strong sense of community, everyone working together towards a common goal (singing "Kum Ba Yah" optional).

Reversed:
Infighting is the worst. Watch what you tell and to who — does what you're repeating really need to be shared?

Position 9
—Hopes and Fears

Upright:
It is time to let the river of love in your heart flow. If someone is unaware of your feelings, enlighten them.

Reversed
You're backing the wrong horse. Check yourself for misplaced loyalties and see if who you trust is worth it.

Position 10
—The Outcome

Upright:
All's well that ends well — now the lovers kiss and ride off into the glorious sunset. Happy endings all around!

Reversed:
It was nice while it lasted, but now divorce/separation is tearing happiness asunder. See what pieces can be salvaged before moving on.

Pentacles

The Ace of Pentacles

Whenever you see Pentacles in a reading, manifesting your desires into reality—and into cold hard cash—are featured in the center ring. This Ace invites you to get fired up and ready; opportunity is about to coming a'knocking.

Meaning in a Nutshell:
Potential

Position 1—The Situation

Upright:
You've been sitting around talking about it long enough—time to get your potential on and strut your stuff.

Reversed:
If you're even thinking about taking a gamble, you've got more thinking to do. Too much risk involved with whatever you're considering.

Position 2

—The Crossing

Upright:
Heads up: a plum of an opportunity is going to fall right in your waiting lap. Keep your eyes open.

Reversed:
The current climate smells like a get-rich scheme. If it sounds too good to be true—run. Far away. Fast.

Position 3—The Base

Upright:
Get ready for a change in luck—a shiny new period of prosperity is riding shotgun beside you. Use it wisely.

Reversed:
Good resources are hard to come by. Don't squander yours on nonessentials until you get your financial bearings.

Position 4—The Past

Upright:
There may have been a career change or maybe just a change in perspective. Either way, change was good.

Reversed:
Hasty decisions lead to shaky situations. You may have spoken or acted without thinking. No turning back now, though.

Position
—The Crowning

Upright:
Now is the time to get your head on straight and think practically. Plot your strategy. Get your game plan on.

Reversed:
Best look at those shiny pretty enticements closely—underneath you'll find they're not all they're cracked up to be.

Position 6
—The Future

Upright:
You've got good hunches. If you're thinking of taking a chance, this might be your hoped-for opportunity.

Reversed:
You'll never get anywhere if you're afraid of change, but this isn't the time to tackle that fear. Stay put.

Position 7—The Self

Upright:
No one can accuse you of being vague. You are sincere in your beliefs and are trustworthy to a fault.

Reversed:
Carelessness is a sign that you aren't putting in enough time to get the results you want. Slow down.

Position 8
—Outside Influences

Upright:
You've got plenty of helping hands to assist you towards your goal. Take advantage of their offered experience.

Reversed:
Some promises are made with no intent of ever making good. If you're on the receiving end, don't expect much.

Position 9
—Hopes and Fears

Upright:
Material gain in any form—be it winning the lottery or just finding a dollar—is good. Use yours wisely.

Reversed:
Greed is unattractive, literally. Don't think about how much you don't have unless you really don't want to have it.

Position 10
—The Outcome

Upright:
You are on the fast track to making your goals happen. Good planning and execution will see you go far.

Reversed:
Scared money never wins. Don't take a risk unless you are willing and able to lose your stake.

The Two of Pentacles

This or that, either/or: this Two is a balancing act. When it appears in a reading, look for two (sometimes more) obligations or choices to be weighing heavily upon you. How long can you keep the balls in the air, Juggler?

Meaning in a Nutshell:
Balance

Position 1—The Situation

Upright:
Some say that those who remain flexible don't get bent out of shape. You should say—and do—just that.

Reversed:
You're being bombarded from every direction you turn. Sometime TMI (too much information) really isn't a good thing.

Position 2 —The Crossing

Upright:
Pretend you're a chameleon and see how quickly you can adapt to your new environment. Roll with the changes.

Reversed:
Tend to your responsibilities before they get completely out of hand. You're unable to complete the tasks you've already started, so don't take on any new ones.\

Position 3—The Base

Upright:
You're spreading yourself a little too thin these days. If you're not careful, everything will suffer as a result.

Reversed:
Impulsive, you are it. Learn to think about what you're saying before the fact and look up the meaning of NO.

Position 4—The Past

Upright:
You've been way preoccupied with money matters, mostly how to get more of it. Thinking outside the norms would help.

Reversed:
Just like the grasshopper of fable, you squandered your wealth without a care for the future. You're paying for that now.

The Two of Pentacles

Position —The Crowning

Upright:
You need to work on conquering the time management monster. Learn to budget minutes as well as money.

Reversed:
Back away slowly from the (insert cool electronic toy here). Get out in the real world for a while—it's missed you.

Position 6—The Future

Upright:
Borrowing from Peter to pay Paul is no way to make ends meet. Better come up with another plan to stay afloat.

Reversed:
You're overwhelmed, buried under an avalanche of paperwork and red tape. You can dig your way out with patience.

Position 7—The Self

Upright:
A little creative bookkeeping can be acceptable from time to time, but don't make a habit of bending the numbers.

Reversed:
If you live only in the moment, don't be surprised when the moment you live in passes you by.

Position 8 —Outside Influences

Upright:
Your social calendar might read like a cruise ship itinerary, but there's only so many hours in the day. Slow down.

Reversed:
If you're only trying to keep up appearances, who are you cheating in the long run? Hint: it's you.

Position 9 —Hopes and Fears

Upright:
Know that you're in it for the long haul. You've got more stamina than you're giving yourself credit for.

Reversed:
Debt is like mold—creeps in when you're not looking. Start with the little ones to work your way up and out.

Position 10 —The Outcome

Upright:
You can get it all done and come out smelling like a rose—do what you must, delegate what you can.

Reversed:
You're taking too many unnecessary chances and your reckless attitude will land you in even more hot water.

The Three of Pentacles

The master craftsman takes a lot of deserved pride in his work—took a lot of practice to get him there. This Three tells you to be proud of your accomplishments, but don't think you don't have anything more to learn.

Meaning in a Nutshell:
Mastery

Position 1—The Situation

Upright:
You've got the talent to make a real difference, but it is the utilization of said talent at issue.

Reversed:
Now isn't the time to be meek and mild, so step up and assert yourself before some else does.

Position 2 —The Crossing

Upright:
Your teacher is coming. They may not see themselves as such, but you will be learning much from them nonetheless.

Reversed:
Not everyone who touts themselves as an expert really is. Ask for credentials and references before buying into their spiel.

Position 3—The Base

Upright:
Holding yourself to a higher standard is what will shape and define you, setting you apart from the competition.

Reversed:
You need a helping hand from an outside source, someone who has been in your position before and knows what to do.

Position 4—The Past

Upright:
You've got a reputation for seeing things a bit differently. Innovation is truly the spark of genius at work.

Reversed:
Just because you've always done it that way doesn't mean the process can't be improved with a little ambition.

Position —The Crowning

Upright:
You've got some well-deserved distinction and fame coming—get ready to bask in the glow of your awesomeness.

Reversed:
It's good to stay focused but don't lapse into tunnel vision. See the big picture, not just the desired outcome.

Position 6—The Future

Upright:
Sharpen your skills and be ready to work. Go for quality instead of flash—it is better in the long run.

Reversed:
You might want to rethink this—you don't have all the tools necessary to do the job you're contemplating.

Position 7—The Self

Upright:
Do it right or not at all—your refusal to accept anything less than your best is the best advertisement.

Reversed:
Don't let pettiness cause you to tear your competition down. Be courteous, gracious, and confident in your own abilities.

Position 8 —Outside Influences

Upright:
You're no stranger to hard work. Roll up your sleeves and get busy. Recruit some like-minded people to help.

Reversed:
Your ideas are meeting with strong opposition; you're not just imagining it. It's less controversial to blend right now.

Position 9 —Hopes and Fears

Upright:
You're looking for visible results in your craft, proof positive of your peer's respect. Remember your work doesn't define you.

Reversed:
You're not giving 100% of your effort and it shows. Try a little harder and you'll see the results you desire.

Position 10 —The Outcome

Upright:
You have the tools and talent, the knowledge and know how. Rewards are yours for a job well done.

Reversed:
It is time to head back to school for more lessons. You're not quite ready for the big time yet.

The Four of Pentacles

Bigger, better, faster, more—this Four wants it all. The more you get, the more you want. Although cool toys are loads of fun, remember that what you own doesn't define you—it's who you are inside that counts.

Meaning in a Nutshell:
Acquisition

Position 1—The Situation

Upright:
Your need for financial security is first and foremost on the agenda, driving you to hard decisions about spending.

Reversed:
You're going to need to look past your own needs for a minute and focus on the bigger picture.

Position 2
—The Crossing

Upright:
Fear of loss is greater than the desire for gain. Don't let it push you into unwise business transactions.

Reversed:
Take any investment advice with a grain of salt. Small, baby steps are the way to build your fortune.

Position 3—The Base

Upright:
You need to protect your own territory by keeping a sharp eye out. Don't' trust others to do it for you.

Reversed:
Money, money, money—your obsession is blinding you to more important, less tangible aspects of living the fullest life.

Position 4—The Past

Upright:
You may have gone wanting in the past and you remember what it's like. Keep in touch with your humble roots.

Reversed:
You may not have had it all, but you had more than your share. Learn to appreciate what you were given.

Position —The Crowning

Upright:
You don't have a fear of change; you'd just rather get paid in paper money. Keep your expectations realistic.

Reversed:
Rather than focusing on just you, try seeing what would be in the highest good for all concerned.

Position 6—The Future

Upright:
Your reluctance to take a risk says it's better to make a slow nickel than a fast dime. Good, safe thinking.

Reversed:
You've got yourself hemmed in by outmoded thinking. Don't confine your creativity to ideals past their expiration date.

Position 7—The Self

Upright:
Just because you don't want to share, you're taking all your toys home. How about loosening your grasp a bit?

Reversed:
Paranoia will creep up on you if you're not careful—but don't be paranoid. Just relax and try to stay calm.

Position 8 —Outside Influences

Upright:
If you have questions, just ask. People will happily offer advice if you act like you're open to suggestion.

Reversed:
You are the star on your team of one. Trying letting others help you carry the load for a while.

Position 9 —Hopes and Fears

Upright:
Your suspicions may or may not be founded in reality, but your stinginess is, Mr. Scrooge. Lighten up.

Reversed:
Having finally gotten off the porch, you're running with the big dogs, the movers and shakers. Yeah You!

Position 10 —The Outcome

Upright:
You're guarding your assets more fiercely than a dragon with treasure. It's great, but that's not all there is to life.

Reversed:
Money isn't everything, but it does help. Good, sound financial advice and management will get you ahead in the game.

The Five of Pentacles

Nobody knows the trouble I've seen…except the Five of Pentacles. You had it all; you lost it all. Struggles and hardship are the order of the day. Fives are change, however, so it won't always be this way.

Meaning in a Nutshell:
Want

Position 1—The Situation

Upright:
Financial problems loom dark and gloomy on the horizon, so heed the storm clouds and starting preparing now.

Reversed:
Things have been looking pretty bleak for a while, but your luck might be taking a turn for the better.

Position 2—The Crossing

Upright:
Money problems and overspending is at the root of the problem. Take "charge it" out of your vocabulary.

Reversed:
Don't be so proud that you can't accept the hand of charity extended to you. There's no shame in needing help.

Position 3—The Base

Upright:
Nobody knows you when you're down and out, especially if you're trying to borrow money. Learn to make do with less.

Reversed:
Hard times are coming to an end, but don't use that as an excuse to squander what little you currently have.

Position 4—The Past

Upright:
Self doubt is a self fulfilling prophecy. If you don't believe in yourself, no one else will either.

Reversed:
You never were one to worry about the future. It's hard to think of rain when the sun is shining.

Position

—The Crowning

Upright:
When you've lost hope, you've lost everything. Everything is temporary, but things have to get worse before they get better.

Reversed:
If you were looking to make a clean break and start over, this is the time. Don't look back.

Position 6—The Future

Upright:
Worry is mental cancer and should be avoided. Cross those scary bridges when you come to them, not before.

Reversed:
You've come to a safe haven, a place to rest while you recover. Don't forget to say a heartfelt thank you.

Position 7—The Self

Upright:
You're consumed with self pity. Do you think you'd heal faster if no one was around to hear you complain?

Reversed:
If you save those pennies, they add up in no time. Plan your purchases, stick to the list, and spend wisely.

Position 8

—Outside Influences

Upright:
If you think you can't, you're absolutely right—you can't. Don't get caught up in everyone else's fatalistic thinking.

Reversed:
Your circle of loved ones is waiting to welcome you back into the fold with open arms—go, already.

Position 9

—Hopes and Fears

Upright:
Despondency can drag you down into full-on depression. Lighten up and laugh a little—this too shall pass.

Reversed:
A fresh start is on the horizon if that's what you're looking for. Don't make the same mistakes next time.

Position 10

—The Outcome

Upright:
The demands for sympathy are becoming tiresome, not to mention increasingly irritating. Quit complaining and so something about the problem.

Reversed:
It's a bright new day and yours to do with as you will. You're getting a second chance so use it wisely.

The Six of Pentacles

Charity is giving when you can spare it, true giving is doing it when you can't. This Six says the best giving is done in secret. Pay it forward and the rewards will come back to you when you least expect it.

Meaning in a Nutshell:
Benevolence

Position 1—The Situation

Upright:
It is better to give than receive. Get in the habit of not expecting something in return—you'll be happier.

Reversed:
Watch out for those needing an audience for their good works. Their motives are not on the up and up.

Position 2—The Crossing

Upright:
This is a good opportunity to share the wealth. Remember when you were on the receiving end and be gracious.

Reversed:
You may be in a position of authority, but don't flex your managerial muscles just for the sake of showing off.

Position 3—The Base

Upright:
The best good deeds are those done anonymously and the best giving has no strings attached.

Reversed:
Blowing your resources on meaningless pursuits is wasteful, considering all the good you could do with them.

Position 4—The Past

Upright:
You've been shown kindness and compassion. Remember how it made you feel? You can give that feeling to someone in need.

Reversed:
You've been kept down, your submission demanded by circumstance. Never forget how it feels to be backed into a corner.

Position —The Crowning

Upright:
Your material needs are being met on a grand scale. Don't ask for more than your share, take only what is needed.

Reversed:
Refusing to help those in need will come back to bite you. Think long and hard before choosing that path.

Position 6—The Future

Upright:
Begin practicing random acts of kindness—once sown, those seeds bloom in the most unexpected and delightful places.

Reversed:
If you have unpaid debts floating around, you're on notice that they will soon be called due. Ready your checkbook.

Position 7—The Self

Upright:
Learn to empathize rather than sympathize with others. Feel what it's like to be someone else, to walk in their shoes.

Reversed:
It's all about you, you, you—NOT. Your attitude holds you back, keeping you in a state of arrested development.

Position 8 —Outside Influences

Upright:
Get those financial molehills taken care of before they turn into mountains. Get qualified advice if you need help.

Reversed:
You've got a lot of friends around, at least until the first sign of stormy weather. Careful who you trust.

Position 9 —Hopes and Fears

Upright:
Now is a good time to write out your financial goals; then create the action plan to make them happen.

Reversed:
You might notice things have grown legs and left lately—there is a thief at work. Watch your stuff closely.

Position 10 —The Outcome

Upright:
You're about to be recognized for your accomplishments. Give credit where credit is due—you couldn't have done it alone.

Reversed:
You're firmly under someone else's thumb for the moment. It won't be your time to shine until you break loose.

The Seven of Pentacles

This is the pause that refreshes. The Seven tells you it's time to take stock, see where you've been and where you're headed. Don't stop for too long, though, lest you lose momentum and forget to get started again.

**Meaning in a Nutshell:
Reflection**

Position 1—The Situation

Upright:
Take a deep breath and relax a moment. You've come a long way, but still have further to go.

Reversed:
You're high, you're low—a little consistency would be nice. Find the midway point between the two and stay there.

Position 2
—The Crossing

Upright:
Just like the fable, slow and steady wins the race. Be persistent and above all patient. You'll get there.

Reversed:
This is the bad gambler's card—don't do anything without thinking long and hard about it first. Then think some more.

Position 3—The Base

Upright:
Do you really have all that much to do or is it a fear of success that has you hesitating?

Reversed:
Don't let a little adversity make you quit—you're giving up and throwing in the towel way too easily.

Position 4—The Past

Upright:
You've done a lot of work. You've invested wisely and are now seeing the results of your efforts.

Reversed:
Got a bad case of disillusionment? Seems like nothing is ever as good as we want it to be.

Position —
Crowning Card

Upright:
It's better to make a slow nickel than a fast dime. Take your time building the foundation for your business.

Reversed:
Cutting corners and taking shortcuts isn't the way to succeed. You lose time having to do things over.

Position 6—The Future

Upright:
Keep evaluating and tweaking your process—the journey is a constant series of little adjustments, not a straight line.

Reversed:
Procrastination is a time stealer. Cross your fingers that it won't be too late when you finally get around to it.

Position 7—The Self

Upright:
Time flies when you're focused on working towards a desired goal. You're paying "those working for a living" dues.

Reversed:
Life has become setback after setback. Take it one fire at a time, putting out each as they pop up.

Position 8
—Outside Influences

Upright:
Don't feel like you have to make all the hard decisions on your own. Consult with others, get their feedback.

Reversed:
You're not carrying your share of the load. It's not fair to the others who are and will cause resentment.

Position 9
—Hopes and Fears

Upright:
Before you take one more step, you better think about the consequences of your actions. There will be some.

Reversed:
Inattention to important matters will bring nothing but extended heartache. Do the critical needs stuff first, no matter how unpleasant.

Position 10
—The Outcome

Upright:
Step back for a moment and take a look at the big picture. Remember it? Good. Now get back to work.

Reversed:
Don't let your mistakes be a waste of effort. Learn from them so that they are not repeated.

The Eight of Pentacles

Taking care of business—this Eight is on the j-o-b. Cross the "t's" and dot every "i"; it's the attention to detail that will get you noticed. Put in those long hours now and you'll reap the rewards later.

Meaning in a Nutshell:
Productivity

Position 1—The Situation

Upright:
Focused effort is going to get you the attention and notice you're looking for. Eyes on the prize, please.

Reversed:
All the know-how in the world isn't going to help you if you're not prepared to do the job.

Position 2
—The Crossing

Upright:
Never miss an opportunity to learn, even if it's from a bad example. Take notes if you need to.

Reversed:
You are failing to follow through. Make time to take care of the details; they'll come back to haunt you later.

Position 3—The Base

Upright:
Focus on quality, not quantity. You'd rather be associated with craftsmanship and expertise, not mass production of inferior products.

Reversed:
Nobody owes you anything. It doesn't matter what you did before, it's what you've done lately that is important.

Position 4—The Past

Upright:
It's always a test of nerve when you attempt a new line of work. Your bravery has carried the day.

Reversed:
Poor job performance has a ripple effect—it impacts everyone around you. Learn to carry your share of the load.

Position

—The Crowning

Upright:
If it is a teacher you want, make yourself ready, and when it is time, he/she will come to you.

Reversed:
You only put in a half-hearted, second-rate effort. It's no surprise that you got the same as a result.

Position 6—The Future

Upright:
No one ever stays the same. You either get better or worse and (hint) you have to work to get better.

Reversed:
You can't wheel-and-deal your way to the top—your lack of experience will expose you as a fraud.

Position 7—The Self

Upright:
You've got the needed talent and skill. Be proactive and work out the details of your development plan.

Reversed:
You might really be the best thing since sliced bread, but if you can't back it up it's all just bragging.

Position 8

—Outside Influences

Upright:
Take initiative—put in the extra effort to do a great job before you're asked. You'll stay under the boss's radar.

Reversed:
There is a place for everything and everything should be in its place. All the time. No exceptions. Ever.

Position 9

—Hopes and Fears

Upright:
No one is going to put you in charge unless you earn the right to be there. Pay your dues.

Reversed:
You've got the dreams, just not the capital to make them come true. Try a different, less costly approach.

Position 10

—The Outcome

Upright:
You already know what you have to be and do in order to meet your goals—as you were, soldier.

Reversed:
You've got great skill and energy, but both are pointed in the wrong direction. Time to reevaluate the master plan.

The Nine of Pentacles

Nine is the number of material surplus. Those luxuries you're enjoying – you earned 'em. Kick back, relax, and enjoy the fruits of your labor. If the labor wasn't as fruitful as you'd like, make notes on what to do different next time.

Meaning in a Nutshell: Independence

Position 1—The Situation

Upright:
Calm, cool, and collected – that's you. You ooze self-confidence and command attention wherever you go. Make it work for you.

Reversed:
You're a lot stronger than you give yourself credit for. You don't need to be so dependent on others.

Position 2 —The Crossing

Upright:
You may be the recipient of a surprise, either a gift or some good news you weren't expecting. Enjoy the moment!

Reversed:
Keep your eyes open – the theft may not be obvious, so watch out for small pilferages. They add up quickly.

Position 3—The Base

Upright:
The sun is shining and life is good. Appreciate all the blessings showered down on you, show a little gratitude.

Reversed:
Bad money management is the author of your current sorrows. Make a budget and stick to it in the future.

Position 4—The Past

Upright:
You were in the right place at the right time and your gambles paid off. Your instincts were spot-on target.

Reversed:
Decisions made in haste are seldom good. Jumping the gate before the starting pistol fired didn't help you at all.

Position —The Crowning

Upright:
Enjoy those luxuries you've worked hard for. There's a little more work to do, but you've earned a break.

Reversed:
Lose that sense of entitlement — you only get what you earn. Don't stand around waiting with your hand out.

Position 6—The Future

Upright:
If you use your talents wisely, you can secure your financial future. Watch out for good investment opportunities.

Reversed:
Your integrity is being questioned — remember that to some, being *thought* a crook and *being* a crook are the same thing.

Position 7—The Self

Upright:
You are the picture of refinement — nothing but the best for you. You have an air of class and sophistication.

Reversed:
Three year olds have the luxury of being totally self-indulgent. It is a less attractive quality in a grownup.

Position 8 —Outside Influences

Upright:
If you're not up on your networking skills, now is the time to dust them off. Get out there, make contacts.

Reversed:
Not everyone being friendly is a friend. Same goes for enemies. Don't get attached to any friendships made right now.

Position 9 —Hopes and Fears

Upright:
You are all set materially, but not emotionally. What good is wealth if there's no one to share it with?

Reversed:
Barely making ends meet is a miserable way to go through life. Look at your expenses for frivolous spending.

Position 10 —The Outcome

Upright:
There's no greater satisfaction than knowing that you are able to take care of yourself...a noble goal, to be sure.

Reversed:
Scruples and sound, moral judgment seem to be in short supply these days. Rent some if you don't have any.

The Ten of Pentacles

This Ten is the card of inheritances passed from generation to generation. What legacy are you leaving for those who come after you? Even if it's just planting a tree, do something from which you'll never see the benefit.

Meaning in a Nutshell:
Legacy

Position 1—The Situation

Upright:
Yours has been a life of privilege. Even if you haven't gone without, get some empathy for those who haven't.

Reversed:
You've forgotten—or you're ignoring—where you've come from. Denying your family roots doesn't change the facts of their existence.

Position 2—The Crossing

Upright:
Having a healthy outlook on the past is a good foundation for the future. You are being rewarded for your contributions.

Reversed:
Be careful gambling or otherwise risking your financial stake. You may have legal problems lurking just around the corner.

Position 3—The Base

Upright:
Now that your goal of financial security is assured, take time to appreciate what your family unit means to you.

Reversed:
Everyone has skeletons in their closet. Don't be ashamed of yours—dress them up and take them out to play.

Position 4—The Past

Upright:
Old money sometimes equals old ways of thinking. Don't get stuck in a rut—try new things and experiment a little.

Reversed:
No family is perfect—every group has its internal squabbles and differences. Don't take it so deeply to heart.

Position —The Crowning

Upright:
You're coming into your inheritance. It might not be cold, hard cash, but there are things more important than money.

Reversed:
You've got more than your share of responsibilities and they are weighing heavily upon you. Don't worker harder, work smarter.

Position 6—The Future

Upright:
With success comes stability, something your life has been lacking lately. See if you can adjust to the "drama-free zone."

Reversed:
Some would say you've got more money than sense. Don't invest your resources without getting value in return.

Position 7—The Self

Upright:
Some say you're old fashioned, but you can't change who you are. The Boy Scouts think you're a great role model.

Reversed:
Holding a grudge uses up gray matter that could be put to better use. Don't waste your energy on them.

Position 8 —Outside Influences

Upright:
Listen to your elders—even if you think they're out of date. They've usually been there, done that, bought the shirt.

Reversed:
The pressures of family obligations are making you grit your teeth. No getting out of the responsibilities, though.

Position 9 —Hopes and Fears

Upright:
Give a little thought to where you'll be five, ten, and twenty years from now. Start planning accordingly.

Reversed:
Your financial platform is a lot on the shaky side. Better get your cash flow in order before making big plans.

Position 10 —The Outcome

Upright:
Remember that you are part of a legacy and conduct yourself as a proud part of that longstanding tradition.

Reversed:
Spoiled much? You could do a lot more with a lot less. Don't let resentment affect your good judgment.

The Tarot Court

Shudder

There's not a Tarot reader alive who doesn't get the slightest urge to run screaming whenever one of these cards appear. (Helpful hint: try not to do that, especially if you're reading for someone else. It stresses them out and blows any credibility you may have built up).

Each member of the Court has a distinct personality with specific quirks and traits. Whenever you see one of these in a reading, it is for one of these reasons:

A. This is the general mood or attitude affecting the situation.
B. This is the general mood or attitude displayed by the querent (person asking the question).
C. This is the general mood or attitude the querent needs to adopt to get through the current situation.
D. The card represents an actual person involved in the situation.

Tricky, right? Yes, but you CAN get through it.

The suits will be introduced one by one, telling you a little about the members so you can get to know them better. Read through each one, paying particular note to the personality traits that will apply either to A, B, C, or D (see prior). You'll need to use your noggin on this one. For example, if your question is about love/romance and you draw the Page of Pentacles reversed as a Crossing Card, it's going to be up to you to determine how to apply the character traits of carelessness and inattention to detail to your question.

Now that you've got the general idea, meet the family.

The Tarot Court is divided into four groups:

Kings, Queens, Knights, and Pages

Kings and Queens are generally mature men and women over the age of thirty. They can represent authority figures or situations where you have to deal with those in positions of power.

Knights are younger adults and can be male or female. While they take on the characteristics of their parents, they're not mature enough yet to always make the right choices. Knights can also indicate where fresh energy is needed.

Pages are children and almost always associated with messages, information, or breaking news. Pages can be either sex.

Swords

The Swords are typically presented as people with dark brown to black hair, dark eyes, and olive skin OR associated with the Air signs of Libra, Aquarius, or Gemini.

The Page of Swords

This little darling is the wunderkind or prodigy of the Tarot, dexterous and quick. On the other hand, he knows it. He's a little bit of a brat and not above spying to further his position. Look for messages in writing.

Meaning in a Nutshell:
Analyze

Position 1—The Situation

Upright:
You act decisively and swiftly, making everything look so easy. Yours is an easy confidence, born of practice and skill.

Reversed:
Rebel without a cause or rebel without a clue—either way, you're going against the accepted status quo.

Position 2—The Crossing

Upright:
Nothing wrong with being inquisitive, but you know what they say about curiosity and the cat. Be careful.

Reversed:
You may be acting like a spoiled child, self-indulgent and self-consumed. Mind your own business.

Position 3—The Base

Upright:
You're so strong willed - don't be so intent on getting your own way that you don't listen to potentially useful advice.

Reversed:
Someone's got secrets that they're not telling. Don't take anything at face value without a little investigation first.

Position 4—The Past

Upright:
You've always found yourself up to mental challenges. If you didn't know the answer, you knew where to look.

Reversed:
There may be psychological abuse in the past, but that has been overcome. It didn't kill you—it made you stronger.

Position —The Crowning

Upright:
You've got a unique style all your own. All eyes are upon you, so flaunt it—it's your time to shine.

Reversed:
You're too clever for your own good. Try being a little more compassionate and a little less smug about it.

Position 6—The Future

Upright:
Diplomacy? It's your middle name. Yours is the voice of reason in the midst of madness, the one they'll listen to.

Reversed:
If you have to ask "what's in it for me?" then your motives aren't purely altruistic. Don't fake your sincerity.

Position 7—The Self

Upright:
You've got enough energy to light a small city. It's focusing it in one direction that's the challenge.

Reversed:
Just like Veruca Salt, your demanding behavior is going to land you in hot water, if not the garbage chute.

Position 8 —Outside Influences

Upright:
You have what it takes to be a skilled negotiator, able to see both sides without taking either.

Reversed:
Gossiping will come back to haunt you if you indulge in it. Keep your ears open, but mind your own business.

Position 9 —Hopes and Fears

Upright:
Your discriminating intellect is a valuable tool—you can tell the difference between a good fake and the real deal.

Reversed:
Vindictive behavior and plotting revenge only hurts *you*, not your intended target. Take a deep breath and relax. Let it go.

Position 10 —The Outcome

Upright:
What may seem daring to others is only a calculated risk for you. Fortunes are both made and lost with boldness.

Reversed:
You've got a handy-dandy excuse and every reason under the sun why you're not responsible. Accept your share, please.

The Page of Swords

The Knight of Swords

The keeper of order, this Knight will use his considerable power to influence people and further his agenda. He is courageous and determined, but can also be ruthless and arrogant—you definitely want to stay on this guy's good side.

Meaning in a Nutshell: Aggression

Position 1—The Situation

Upright:
You're receiving a call to arms—whatever you've been doing before, stop. It's time to stop talking and act.

Reversed:
You wield your power like a sword in your efforts to make sure everyone knows you're taking control of the situation.

Position 2—The Crossing

Upright:
Your ambition is apparent; you wear it on your shoulder like a chip. Be careful who you trample in its pursuit.

Reversed:
Watch heavy handedness. A complete disregard for others has a bad habit of biting you when you least expect it.

Position 3—The Base

Upright:
You are the warrior prince, fired up in pursuit of a noble cause. Get ready to lead your troops into battle.

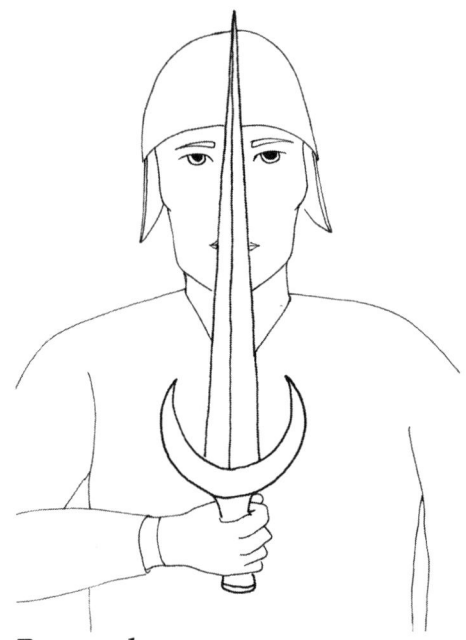

Reversed:
Intolerance and impatience do more harm than good in leading others. Set a good example and they will follow.

Position 4—The Past

Upright:
You've gotten a reputation as a problem solver, a real go-to person when things get difficult and sticky.

Reversed:
Playing one person against another isn't a good modus operandi—dabbling in intrigue is a very dangerous game.

Position
—The Crowning

Upright:
Yours is true power. You've got assertiveness down to an art form, knowing what you want and how to get it.

Reversed:
The burning desire to win at any cost is dehumanizing. Every little compromise eats a tiny bit of soul.

Position 6—The Future

Upright:
Brute strength won't get you anywhere this time; the situation requires finesse and expertise to sooth the savage beasties.

Reversed:
Beware of hidden agendas and strange bedfellows—there is more going on here than meets the eye.

Position 7—The Self

Upright:
You are as focused as it is possible to be. Your level of determination to succeed is commendable.

Reversed:
There is a fine line between confidence and conceit. Be sure to watch for it when you're talking about yourself.

Position 8
—Outside Influences

Upright:
You're got real leadership material and it hasn't gone unnoticed. Prepare to be recognized for your efforts and achievements.

Reversed:
There are those who would stoop to any level to get what they want. Don't fall into that category.

Position 9
—Hopes and Fears

Upright:
There's a heart beating somewhere inside you; you just need to reconnect with it. Don't dismiss your emotions out of hand.

Reversed:
False bravado will only take you so far. There's no shame in admitting you need a little help.

Position 10
—The Outcome

Upright:
Your logical methods are needed to get to the heart of the matter. Full speed ahead and damn the torpedoes!

Reversed:
Your grip on the situation is too tight for anyone to get a breath. Relax a bit—nobody likes a tyrant.

The Queen of Swords

The Queen amazes you with her perceptive observations—don't think to trick her because she definitely won't be tricked. She could smile a little more often, having seen her share of sadness. She suffers no fools gladly, so tread lightly around her.

Meaning in a Nutshell:
Astute

Position 1—The Situation

Upright:
She is Woman, hear her roar. In complete control, she oozes confidence and competence with every fiber of her being.

Reversed:
She lets bitterness get the better of her. Cold and calculating, she will stop at nothing to get what she wants.

Position 2—The Crossing

Upright:
It's okay to be outspoken if you have something worth saying. Keep your eyes, ears, and mind open wide.

Reversed:
Caution: Bitch on wheels at twelve o'clock. Considered to be armed and dangerous. Proceed at your own risk.

Position 3—The Base

Upright:
Don't put up with silliness you're not in the mood for, especially if it doesn't further you towards your goal.

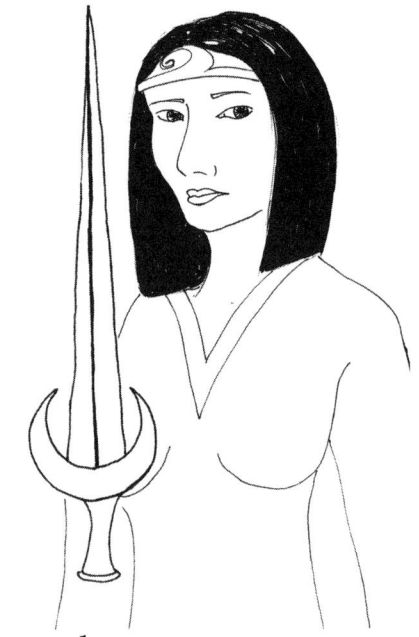

Reversed:
Some situations require nerves of steel to get through. Be careful that you don't have a heart to match.

Position 4—The Past

Upright:
You've learned that sometimes it's easier to get through troubles if you can just shut down, emotionally distancing yourself.

Reversed:
Your unforgiving nature has dug a hole so deep that you can't get out. Don't be afraid to admit you're wrong.

Position —The Crowning

Upright:
You're a survivor, one who has lived through tough situations. Be proud of your battle scars—you've earned them.

Reversed:
Be very careful whose bad side you get on—there is a formidable enemy lurking just outside your castle walls.

Position 6—The Future

Upright:
It's all right; you've got this. It has come down to a battle of wills. Remember that he who blinks first loses.

Reversed:
If you feel you're being manipulated, look up to see who holds the strings. It might surprise you.

Position 7—The Self

Upright:
No man—or woman—is an island. You can be solitary by nature and still socialize once in a while.

Reversed:
Being angry all the time burns a lot of energy you could better use elsewhere. Calm down. Breathe. Repeat.

Position 8 —Outside Influences

Upright:
You've got your own ideas about where you should be. Enlist others to aid you in your quest for glory.

Reversed:
Judgmental to a fault, you jump to conclusions and make assumptions. Listen to the whole story before forming your opinion.

Position 9 —Hopes and Fears

Upright:
Your keen powers of observation will serve you well. Pay extra attention to the subtle changes going on.

Reversed:
Intolerance is a hard—and unpopular—position to take. Try to be a little more accepting of those different from you.

Position 10 —The Outcome

Upright:
Your reputation of being fair and impartial will put you center stage. Hear all sides of the argument before reading the verdict.

Reversed:
It's one thing to gracefully disagree, quite another to be bitter and vindictive about it. Make sure you aren't overreacting.

The Queen of Swords

The King of Swords

This King rules with a firm and just hand, but don't think you can appeal to his kinder, gentler nature if you screw up—he doesn't have one. When he is angry, he is the Master of Disaster, the Demolition Man.

**Meaning in a Nutshell:
Decisive**

Position 1—The Situation

Upright:
Analytical to the core, you need look at every single aspect before drawing conclusions or making assumptions. Ask the hard questions.

Reversed:
There is a real difference between offering up constructive criticism and being hypercritical. No one likes to be micromanaged.

Position 2—The Crossing

Upright:
There is an immediate need for logical thought and reason, and, depending on circumstances, can also be a call to act.

Reversed:
Although you may expect people to bow and scrape to you, not everyone got that memo. Rein it in a bit.

Position 3—The Base

Upright:
Thinking fast on your feet is a skill you want to hone to perfection. It's saved you more than once.

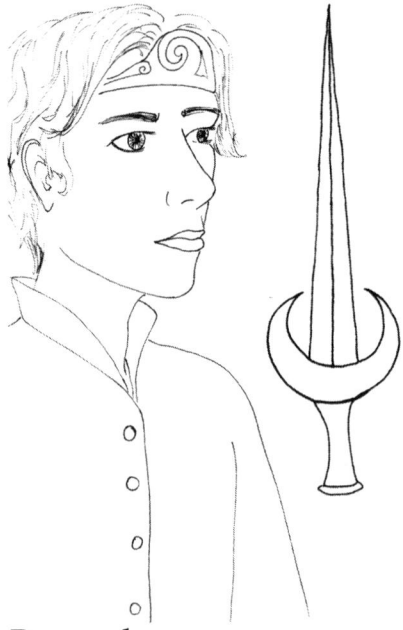

Reversed:
Just because you can't have your own way, there is no reason to be spiteful about it. Channel your kinder, gentler side.

Position 4—The Past

Upright:
Diplomatic to a fault, your impeccable manners have served you well in times of stress. When in doubt, just smile.

Reversed:
It is one thing to be disruptive if there is good reason for it, quite another if you're just bored.

Position
—The Crowning

Upright:
Your strong sense of ethics will lead you to make the right, if not the most politically correct or painless, choice.

Reversed:
The iron fist approach only works if the verdict is fair. Don't abuse your power for your own ends.

Position 6—The Future

Upright:
It's hard to be impartial, especially if you have an interest in a possible outcome. Make the effort, though.

Reversed:
Willows don't get uprooted because they bend with the wind. Stay flexible and keep your roots firmly anchored.

Position 7—The Self

Upright:
You are a very private person. Don't carry the weight of the world by yourself—ask for help if needed.

Reversed:
Not everyone is out to get you, so check the paranoia at the door. Suspicion wastes a lot of good energy.

Position 8
—Outside Influences

Upright:
You have a powerful ally in your corner, one who assures your success and protection on your endeavors.

Reversed:
Someone is acting like a petty tyrant, vengeful and vindictive. Tread lightly. Their power is long reaching and absolute.

Position 9
—Hopes and Fears

Upright:
Don't hold back—grab the bull by those horns and assert yourself. You've got nothing to lose at this point.

Reversed:
Loss of control—you are very afraid of having someone whose opinion does not mirror yours calling all the shots.

Position 10
—The Outcome

Upright:
Temper your control so that it is not so ironclad, as you will find people are more willing to work *with* you than *for* you.

Reversed:
Judge, jury, and executioner: your power is fierce. Take a deep breath and cool off before making any decisions.

Wands

The Wands are typically presented as people with red or fair hair, blue eyes, and fair skin OR associated with the Fire signs of Aries, Leo, or Sagittarius.

The Page of Wands

This is the little darling who wants to strap on a sheet and fly like Superman — preferably off the roof of the house. Definitely one to look before he leaps, he swings between adventurous and foolhardy. Look for messages by phone.

Meaning in a Nutshell: Enthusiasm

Position 1—The Situation

Upright:
The world is a grand adventure to be experienced by those bold enough to dare. What are you waiting for?

Reversed:
You might be getting a little big for your britches. Slow down and get a more realistic vision of your abilities.

Position 2—The Crossing

Upright:
You're generating enough energy to light up a small city. Use it wisely and don't get swept away by exuberance.

Reversed:
Irresponsibility and immaturity go hand-in-hand with a spectacular downfall. Slow down and use the hand rails.

Position 3—The Base

Upright:
You've got to step up your game and seize the moment — grab with both hands and hold on.

Reversed:
Don't be guilty of acting on blind faith alone; keep your eyes open and ask questions if you don't understand.

Position 4—The Past

Upright:
Enterprising and resourceful, you land on your feet and stick the landing when you fall just like a graceful cat.

Reversed:
Your love of a good prank may have landed you in hot water more than once. Learn from past mistakes.

Position —The Crowning

Upright:
You've got a great imagination that will run away if you let it. Keep your head in the game and focus.

Reversed:
Don't get your knickers all in a twist if things don't go exactly how you think they should have.

Position 6—The Future

Upright:
The expression is "full of piss and vinegar." No worries about you—you've got this stuff handled. Watch for incoming messages.

Reversed:
Constancy and you aren't exactly hanging together these days. Quit waffling about important decisions and decide while you still can.

Position 7—The Self

Upright:
No one could ever accuse you of being tepid or dull—you've got enough daring and nerve to face any challenge.

Reversed:
Nobody likes a sore loser, so think before you starting complaining to everyone. You have to work for your win.

Position 8 —Outside Influences

Upright:
Vibrant and outgoing, you are capable of charming the birds right out of the trees when properly motivated.

Reversed:
Others see you as unreliable, vain, and overly dramatic, but you can change their minds if you really want to.

Position 9 —Hopes and Fears

Upright:
Your self-assurance and confidence are contagious—pick your companions wisely as they reflect what you would like to see in yourself.

Reversed:
Being so self-absorbed is bound to backfire on your big plans. Try not worry about getting your due.

Position 10 —The Outcome

Upright:
Your bravura and flair for the dramatic and exciting will take you far. It's an exciting time to be you!

Reversed:
Any which way the wind blows—that's you. Your inability to make a decision is halting progress in its tracks.

The Knight of Wands

Fools and the Knight of Wands rush in where angels fear to tread. "Don't hate the player, hate the game" is this Knight's battle cry. When not pursuing amorous delights, he is the soul of the rebel, the impassioned freedom fighter.

Meaning in a Nutshell:
Idealism

Position 1—The Situation

Upright:
A more passionate person hasn't been born—lover of life and adventure, you have no concept of the word *no*.

Reversed:
A wolf in sheep's clothing, this guy will "paint your face and use you like a fool." He's a true player.

Position 2—The Crossing

Upright:
Like it or not, sweeping change is on your doorstep. Hide the dirty dishes and get ready to welcome it in.

Reversed:
Hot tempered to a fault, you need to cool your jets before you get yourself in a world of trouble.

Reversed:
Headstrong doesn't even come close to describing your level of stubbornness. It's all your way or no way at all.

Position 3—The Base

Upright:
Your enthusiasm knows no bounds, especially if it's something you care deeply about. Try channeling that energy creatively.

Position 4—The Past

Upright:
Your vision of the future included both careful planning and adequate preparation. You didn't leave anything to chance.

Reversed:
If you're looking for a reason for past failure, trying looking closer to home. A little self-discipline would have helped.

Position —The Crowning

Upright:
Don't let the worries of the world dampen your idealistic and noble spirit, let your light shine regardless.

Reversed:
You're letting your hormones dictate your actions and they have no conscience whatsoever. Go take a cold shower instead.

Position 6—The Future

Upright:
Life can be so spontaneous, a brand new adventure every waking moment. Better rest up; things are about to get interesting.

Reversed:
Never one to let a good thing slip past without capitalizing on it, your opportunistic nature is well known.

Position 7—The Self

Upright:
You've got an unsinkable positive attitude—the glass is always half full and the sun will always come up tomorrow.

Reversed:
To say you're a loose cannon is putting it mildly. No one will trust you while you're so unpredictable.

Position 8 —Outside Influences

Upright:
You're a born leader, even if you don't always know where to go. Don't be afraid to ask for directions.

Reversed:
If you have zero tolerance for the differences and opinions of others, don't expect them to accept yours without question.

Position 9 —Hopes and Fears

Upright:
You are a party animal, ready for a day/night of fun without a second thought. Responsibilities? What are those?

Reversed:
Don't volunteer your time or resources if you can't follow through. Road to hell, good intentions—you know the drill.

Position 10 —The Outcome

Upright:
You're an adrenaline junkie in search of the next big adventure. Have fun, remember to breathe, and don't look down.

Reversed:
Being bored is no reason to instigate trouble for your own amusement. Think of the possible repercussions before acting.

The Queen of Wands

This Queen wants all eyes on her, all the time. She is the original drama queen, but also a confident and ferocious businesswoman. Heads up: in readings concerning love interests, her appearance can indicate the "other woman."

Meaning in a Nutshell:
Passion

Position 1—The Situation

Upright:
You've got energy and ambition to spare and, when you're passionate about your subject, you can light up a small city.

Reversed:
Your insatiable need for attention is turning you into a real drama queen. This drags on every else's nerves and energy levels.

Position 2 —The Crossing

Upright:
Successful, competent, and confident—you've got your skills locked, loaded, and at your disposal. Your business acumen is scary good.

Reversed:
No matter what you think, you don't have to be in complete control every waking moment. Your ego is running amuck.

Position 3—The Base

Upright:
You've always been an independent thinker—try looking outside the box for an unconventional answer to your dilemma.

Reversed:
Emotional blackmail is a dangerous way to get what you want. Surely there are better vacations than guilt trips?

Position 4—The Past

Upright:
The practical application of your knowledge combined with past experience has been instrumental in keeping you organized and on schedule.

Reversed:
Your past actions have marked you as self-centered and self-indulgent, but you can act now to turn those opinions around.

Position —The Crowning

Upright:
Fiercely protective of those you love, you can be warm and caring. Few can rival your passionate nature and fiery temperament.

Reversed:
You're turning molehills into mountains. Quit obsessing on the big picture and tend to the details before they get out of hand.

Position 6—The Future

Upright:
Your wit is legendary when the mood suits. Be sure to use your power for good — it's lethal!

Reversed:
Watch what you say — your words and actions may come across as catty and shallow, no matter how justified you feel.

Position 7—The Self

Upright:
Vibrant and versatile, nobody can hold a candle to your ability to roll with the changes. Nothing ruffles your feathers.

Reversed:
You shoot first and ask questions later. Slow down; don't be so quick to judge until you have all the facts.

Position 8 —Outside Influences

Upright:
A born leader, you have no problems being spokesman or at least outspoken. When you talk, people listen.

Reversed:
Your sense of humor is a whole lot left of center. Don't assume everyone else finds it funny.

Position 9 —Hopes and Fears

Upright:
You are courageous, dynamic, and can change at a moment's notice. Reinvent yourself if you don't like what's in the mirror.

Reversed:
That green-eyed monster is taking over your rational mind. Take a deep breath and get some perspective — quickly.

Position 10 —The Outcome

Upright:
Just like moths to a bug zapper, people are attracted to your passion, fire, and your love of life. Flame on!

Reversed:
You're out of control, intolerant, and demanding. Get yourself back in order quickly before someone — likely you — gets hurt.

The King of Wands

Whether The Chosen One or snake oil salesman, this King is larger than life. People are readily influenced by his words and deeds. A born speaker, he can ignite the passions of others and rally support for almost any cause.

Meaning in a Nutshell:
Charisma

Position 1—The Situation

Upright:
Charming and bold, you can take the bull by the horns in any situation you choose—but choose your causes wisely.

Reversed:
Never one to let a slight pass, you won't rest until you either fix it or screw it up beyond all recognition.

Position 2—The Crossing

Upright:
You could sell ice cubes to an Eskimo, given the right incentive. Your powers of persuasion are phenomenal.

Reversed:
You may be coming into unpleasant contact with the biggest megalomaniac you're ever had the displeasure of dealing with.

Position 3—The Base

Upright:
Innovative when you wish to be, your creativity has the masses inspired. Make sure your actions can withstand public scrutiny.

Reversed:
Get off that autocratic high horse you're riding. No one owes you anything. You're not the boss of everyone.

Position 4—The Past

Upright:
You were motivated and inspired by someone you admire greatly. Imitation really is the sincerest form of flattery.

Reversed:
Your pompous and demeaning attitude hasn't won you any friends. Fortunately, there is still time to learn from your mistakes.

Position
—The Crowning

Upright:
Passionate and bold, all eyes are upon you. What can you do with this power you wield over others?

Reversed:
Your impulsive nature has made you undependable and others are aware. Don't bite off more than you can safely chew.

Position 6—The Future

Upright:
Your penchant for taking risks is paying off. You are versatile and can roll with the changes like a true champion.

Reversed:
No one likes a sore loser, especially one in power. Try tempering the ruthlessness with a little humility.

Position 7—The Self

Upright:
You are ambitious, knowing exactly what you want and how you're going to get it. Be decisive and act!

Reversed:
Sarcastic and cynical, your tongue stings like a scorpion. Be careful who you turn that formidable weapon loose on.

Position 8
—Outside Influences

Upright:
You are a strong leader, generous with praise and stingy with criticism. That's why they love you—you are fair.

Reversed:
You always have to have an audience, even for the most mundane tasks. Try to wean yourself off constant adulation.

Position 9
—Hopes and Fears

Upright:
You are an excellent communicator, always knowing just the right words to say. Do you take your own advice, Alice?

Reversed:
If you're not exercising tolerance, don't expect to be shown any. Self righteousness will guarantee you're alone a lot.

Position 10
—The Outcome

Upright:
Your optimism is infectious and your spirit draws others like moths to a flame. Use this power wisely.

Reversed:
You are a fierce and inflexible enemy, bitter when scorned. Relax and accept it—things won't always go your way.

Cups

The Cups are typically presented as people with light/medium brown or blond hair, hazel eyes, and medium skin OR associated with the Water signs of Cancer, Scorpio, or Pisces.

The Page of Cups

This dreamy little darling is the very soul of sensitivity, prone to flights of fancy and imagination. Artistic and intuitive, she wears her heart on her sleeve and likes to escape into her fantasy world. Look for messages by spoken word.

Meaning in a Nutshell:
Sensitive

Position 1—The Situation

Upright:
Your natural disposition is affectionate and loving. As far as you're concerned, there's always a bright side if you look hard enough.

Reversed:
You are stuck in a state of arrested development. Don't dwell on the past, look towards the future for your answers.

Position 2—The Crossing

Upright:
You've got a great imagination. Use it to the full potential to get you out of your latest jam.

Reversed:
You might want to take off those rose-colored glasses and check in with the real world. It's missed you.

Position 3—The Base

Upright:
Your streak of artistic and creative flair needs to be nurtured. Let your inner muse come out to play!

Reversed:
Escapism doesn't help and substance abuse won't solve your problems—they'll still be there when you straighten up.

Position 4—The Past

Upright:
You've always dreamed big, letting your imagination run wild. Past dreams set the stage for future successes.

Reversed:
You might believe it's all about you, but it depends on who you ask. A little tolerance would serve you well.

Position —The Crowning

Upright:
Being introverted isn't a bad thing—just don't go so deep inside that a search party is needed to find you.

Reversed:
Don't let melancholy keep you from enjoying life. Make up your own mind instead of just following the leader.

Position 6—The Future

Upright:
Being a sensitive and caring person are two of your best qualities—keeps you in touch with your humanity.

Reversed:
Nothing like a little high drama to get the blood flowing? Trying taking that extra energy to the gym instead.

Position 7—The Self

Upright:
You have a lot of hidden talents just waiting to be explored. Dig a little; see what's in there.

Reversed:
Impatience never makes anything better. It just makes you harder to be around for any length of time.

Position 8 —Outside Influences

Upright:
Some tasks are better done alone, but don't be adverse to asking for a little help now and then.

Reversed:
Deception is afoot. Don't allow yourself to be easily led. Ask lots of hard questions and listen to the answers.

Position 9 —Hopes and Fears

Upright:
Your emotional side will overbalance your rational side if not held in check. Pause, breathe, and think before you re/act.

Reversed:
Jealousy isn't a fun state to visit, much less live in. Don't let envy wreck your normally sunny outlook.

Position 10 —The Outcome

Upright:
You are so eager to please, but don't let that youthful exuberance be mistaken for being a pushover.

Reversed:
Your reality isn't rooted in reality. Learn to tell the difference between what's real and wishful thinking.

The Knight of Cups

This Prince Charming has a poet's soul and the heart of a hopeful romantic. He means well but sometimes his emotions get in the way. At best he's an ardent lover, at worst a conniving wolf in sheep's clothing.

Meaning in a Nutshell:
Romantic

Position 1—The Situation

Upright:
Romance isn't everything, it's the only thing. Enjoy the heady feelings, but pay attention to where those emotions are leading you.

Reversed:
Someone is not being upfront about their feelings; they're not who they pretend to be. There is emotional manipulation afoot.

Position 2—The Crossing

Upright:
Prince Charming is in the house—only time will tell if all that gold and sparkle are the real thing.

Reversed:
Guard your heart carefully and don't accept face value. There are sharp, wolfish teeth hiding underneath that snowy fleece.

Position 3—The Base

Upright:
This fantasy lover is a dream come true. Enjoy it while it lasts and don't look too close at the minor details.

Reversed:
Immaturity has reared its ugly head, giving the ego an unneeded boost. Conceit is not attractive even if you are gorgeous.

Position 4—The Past

Upright:
Take a moment to reflect and be grateful for the influences that have shaped your life, both good and bad.

Reversed:
If the house was built on false promises and trickery, it's no wonder it tumbled down around your ears.

Position —The Crowning

Upright:
Get in touch with your kinder, gentler side. Unfurl your creativity to the wind. You know, get artsy.

Reversed:
Don't expect a lot of tea and sympathy when you get all moody and temperamental. No one owes you anything.

Position 6—The Future

Upright:
If you were thinking about getting your hopes up and taking a chance romantically, now is the time. Go for it!

Reversed:
Don't fall for those pretty whispered words hook, line, and sinker. Chances are yours aren't the only ears hearing them.

Position 7—The Self

Upright:
Combine your inherent idealism with your imagination and let the two out to play. Who knows what heights you can reach?

Reversed:
Sugar coating the situation isn't helping matters at all. It will only get worse if you don't face the facts.

Position 8 —Outside Influences

Upright:
You are known for your gallant and compassionate nature. Your natural glow draws those who want to be like you.

Reversed:
You're not being realistic. Don't expect others to do all your dirty work if there's nothing in it for them.

Position 9 —Hopes and Fears

Upright:
A knight in shining armor's big metal boots are hard to fill, but you're up to the task. Be the hero!

Reversed:
Self-love is one thing, narcissism quite another. Step down off your pedestal and try putting someone else first for a change.

Position 10 —The Outcome

Upright:
Declarations of love might be coming your way. Be open to the possibilities and embrace the warm, fuzzy feelings.

Reversed:
Careful, your insincerity is showing. Guard your words. Warning: even the most pathological liars started small with eensy-weensy fabrications.

The Queen of Cups

This fey Queen walks the fine line between this world and the next as the most psychic member of the Court. She can be fun, frivolous, and flirtatious, but don't be fooled—get between her and her young, you'll suffer the consequences.

Meaning in a Nutshell:
Intuitive

Position 1—The Situation

Upright:
Nurturing is your middle name. You are the loving mother type, always ready with a kiss and cuddle for life's boo-boo's.

Reversed:
No stranger to emotional manipulation, you wield guild like a sword, depending on which way your mood swings.

Position 2—The Crossing

Upright:
You are accustomed to acting on your intuition. Don't let now be any different—listen to the little voice within.

Reversed:
You have an intricate internal world to escape to when things don't go your way. Just don't stay there too long.

Position 3—The Base

Upright:
Your imagination is amazingly fertile but you're letting it run away with you, thinking the worst of everyone and everything.

Reversed:
You're most dangerous when you're secretive. Irrational fears are getting the best of you—be realistic about what bothers you.

Position 4—The Past

Upright:
You've got the emotional maturity to be secure in your current position and find comfort in your spiritual convictions.

Reversed:
You swallowed the bait hook, line, and sinker. You're too smart to be this gullible. Next time ask more hard questions.

Position
—The Crowning

Upright:
Tender and sensitive, you are loved for your open, generous heart. Ever perceptive, you can read a person like a book.

Reversed:
You are as fickle as the day is long, changing your mind constantly. Flighty doesn't even begin to describe you.

Position 6—The Future

Upright:
Your kindness is legendary. You are gracious and always show patience and caring, even when the recipient isn't very deserving.

Reversed:
Vanity doesn't become you — all that glitter and fluff is just illusion. Look deeper to find the real beauty.

Position 7—The Self

Upright:
Your interest in the occult is more than just a passing fancy. Satisfy the inner cat and appease your curiosity.

Reversed:
Your web of illusion is so well spun, you're starting to believe your own lies. Separate the real from the wishful thinking.

Position 8
—Outside Influences

Upright:
No one can accuse you of being cold and aloof. You have the knack for making strangers feel like cherished friends.

Reversed:
Prickly as a porcupine, your hypersensitivity is keeping you from enjoying life to the fullest. Don't take everything so personally.

Position 9
—Hopes and Fears

Upright:
Your sentimentality is part of your charm. You have the memory of an elephant and never forget a good turn.

Reversed:
Like a crab, you approach things sideways. For a better result, try being a little more straightforward with your expectations.

Position 10
—The Outcome

Upright:
Trust your intuition — the decision you don't have to question is the right one. Let your caring and empathy shine through.

Reversed:
Your head is turned by every morsel of flattery thrown your way. Don't be so eager for all that attention.

The King of Cups

Patron of the arts and lover of the finer things in life, this King is into luxury. He is the consummate father figure, but has a darker side. Providing either succor or seduction (sometimes both), he is the one you don't see coming.

**Meaning in a Nutshell:
Refinement**

Position 1—The Situation

Upright:
Cultured and refined, there isn't much you haven't seen or done. Don't let all that exposure make you jaded.

Reversed:
Everything isn't as it appears—deception is in the air. Someone is much more crafty that they are letting on.

Position 2—The Crossing

Upright:
You are a seasoned diplomat, one who mingles effortlessly between pauper and prince. Your skills are needed now.

Reversed:
There's a sucker born every minute—just like Hannum said: "Someone's about to get fleeced." Make sure it's not you.

Position 3—The Base

Upright:
Cool under fire, your dignity isn't going to let you lose your legendary control in public. You'll wait until you're alone for that.

Reversed:
Your moral fiber has come unraveled. Clean up your act now or run the risk of having it done for you.

Position 4—The Past

Upright:
You have been a supportive friend and ally. People remember your noble actions when you would have been justified behaving otherwise.

Reversed:
As a committed power seeker, your past is riddled with scandal. Time to lie low and let the storm blow over.

Position —The Crowning

Upright:
Your counsel is sought by many—even by those who may seem to make fun of you. Appearances are deceiving.

Reversed:
Violence is never the answer. Use those excellent powers of deduction to figure out another way to make your point.

Position 6—The Future

Upright:
Leave it to you to always find the humor in any situation. Others love listening to your oddball observations.

Reversed:
Well versed in the arts of seduction, you're not above using emotional manipulation if it gets you what you want.

Position 7—The Self

Upright:
You are definitely the ideal partner—romantic and faithful. Be worthy of the trust and faith placed in you.

Reversed:
You're that special kind of neurotic, needing constant reassurance that everything is okay. No, really. It's okay. REALLY.

Position 8 —Outside Influences

Upright:
Not only do you support the arts, you enjoy finding new ways to experience them. Education goes a long way.

Reversed:
Touchy doesn't even begin to describe your hypersensitivity. It is making everyone walk on eggshells around you.

Position 9 —Hopes and Fears

Upright:
You're one of the most upright and trustworthy people anybody knows. Everybody knows you can get the job done.

Reversed:
Vanity is a big problem for you, even more so when there are no mirrors around. Seriously, you look fine—move on.

Position 10 —The Outcome

Upright:
You wouldn't be caught dead being anything less than perfectly poised. Your image as virtuous and chivalrous is important to you.

Reversed:
Stick a pin in that overinflated ego and come back to earth. Your condescending attitude is out of place here.

Pentacles

The Pentacles are typically presented as people with white or dark hair, any color eyes or skin OR associated with the Earth signs of Capricorn, Taurus, or Virgo.

The Page of Pentacles

The scholar of the Court, this little overachiever is the bane of any classroom grading on the curve. She reads textbooks for fun and is unbeatable at Scrabble, but needs to loosen up and have fun. Look for messages by IM/text.

Meaning in a Nutshell:
Practical

Position 1—The Situation

Upright:
You are curious about the world around you. It's okay—step off the sidelines and get into the game.

Reversed:
Living in ignorance is only excusable if you don't know you are. If you do know, there's no excuse.

Position 2—The Crossing

Upright:
There are opportunities at hand that may have far-reaching financial ramifications. Read the fine print before you sign.

Reversed:
Your inattention to detail is going to cost you dearly. Careless is a dangerous way to go through life.

Position 3—The Base

Upright:
Trust you to always be practical and pragmatic. Let your hair down a little—it's okay to experience new things.

Reversed:
Don't let impatience get the best of you—you'll live to regret the havoc those unnecessary mistakes create.

Position 4—The Past

Upright:
Your insight is far reaching, as in looking past the now to the years from now. Good show for planning ahead!

Reversed:
Any winner will tell you to be your own best cheerleader—toot your own horn lest it not get tooted.

Position —The Crowning

Upright:
Thrifty, trustworthy, and determined, you have the makings of success. You just have to want it badly enough to try.

Reversed:
Just because you're not happy about the situation, don't bring the house down with you. Not everyone is a malcontent.

Position 6—The Future

Upright:
The goals you have set for yourself are reasonable and attainable. Now raise the bar and challenge yourself to do more.

Reversed:
You're agreeing to everything too quickly. Read the fine print of the contract and ask questions if you don't understand.

Position 7—The Self

Upright:
You pride yourself on being articulate and well spoken. Your intelligence and education shine through in every single word you speak.

Reversed:
Snobbish and rude, you aren't making any friends with that elitist attitude. Get down off your high horse.

Position 8 —Outside Influences

Upright:
You've got a great reputation—reliable, punctual, and always ready to chip in and shoulder more than your share of the load.

Reversed:
You're up in everybody's business, filling in the blanks when you don't have all the info. Now stop—gossip is bad.

Position 9 —Hopes and Fears

Upright:
Keep an open mind and consider all the possible angles before making a decision, so you don't have to backpedal later.

Reversed:
Disrespectful and disruptive—either of those "diss" words will get you picked last to play. Nobody likes a problem child.

Position 10 —The Outcome

Upright:
You win the award for good citizenship. You are practical, responsible, respectable, and always do the right thing.

Reversed:
You really should pay more attention to what is going on around you—you're missing out on some important stuff.

The Knight of Pentacles

Everyone's favorite Eagle Scout, this Knight readily volunteers his time for worthy causes. When not rescuing cats in trees, he's working in the soup kitchen or picking up trash. Squeaky clean cut or decidedly dull — maybe he's a little of both.

**Meaning in a Nutshell:
Dependable**

Position 1—The Situation

Upright:
People can set their watch by you — once you get into a routine, it's hard to bust you loose.

Reversed:
Yawn. Not much gets you excited. Perhaps your energy levels have dropped into the cellar. Or maybe everything's just boring.

Position 2

—The Crossing

Upright:
Loyal to a fault, you have qualities a boy scout would kill for, figuratively speaking, of course. You abhor violence.

Reversed:
You're not using your imagination and, worse, you could care less. You'd have to perk up to be apathetic.

Position 3—The Base

Upright:
You always take the pragmatic approach — methodical and to the point. Ever think about coloring outside the lines?

Reversed:
You've got a lot to be proud of, but don't get smug. It's irresponsible to think you can't be replaced.

Position 4—The Past

Upright:
Taking a passive role has been your style. You don't act without having thought things through from every possible angle.

Reversed:
Your behavior has been thoroughly irresponsible—you acted only for the moment's gratification with no thought towards potential future repercussions.

Position
—The Crowning

Upright:
You know that perseverance and hard work is the only way to get anything worth having. Your methods are thorough.

Reversed:
There's that sense of entitlement again, clouding up the present situation and making you expect things you didn't earn.

Position 6—The Future

Upright:
You've got stable down pat. Nothing is going to break your stride or slow you down. Unshakeable and unperturbed—that's you.

Reversed:
You pretend to have altruistic motives, but your greed is shining through. Don't let impatience goad you into making mistakes.

Position 7—The Self

Upright:
You're down to earth and easy going—it takes a lot to make you angry. You choose your battles wisely.

Reversed:
You're so afraid of making a wrong move, you're not moving at all. There IS such a thing as being overcautious.

Position 8
—Outside Influences

Upright:
Still waters run deep, as the saying goes. You are recognized as a well-rounded person, albeit understated and self-deprecating.

Reversed:
Your paranoia is running rampant. Watch how you're throwing those accusations around—make sure of your facts before speaking.

Position 9
—Hopes and Fears

Upright:
You have the gift of contentment and the patience of a saint, but don't let others abuse your good nature.

Reversed:
See that rut? It's what you're stuck in. A little less obstinacy would go a lot way towards helping you progress.

Position 10
—The Outcome

Upright:
You are realistic in your expectations and industrious in your pursuit of them. Slow and steady wins the race.

Reversed:
Stubborn trees get uprooted when the wind blows hard. Try not to be so inflexible that the smallest breeze snaps you.

The Queen of Pentacles

Tend the kids, cook, clean, and sparkle like a gem doing it? Organizer of bake sales and gala events, this Queen both is efficient and effervescent. Just follow her directions—to the letter—and you two will get along fine.

Meaning in a Nutshell:
Competent

Position 1—The Situation

Upright:
Capable and competent, you're the manager every CEO dreams about—the auto-pilot employee who doesn't need constant direction.

Reversed:
Ignoring your responsibilities doesn't make you any less obligated for them. Try thinking of the greater good instead of your own wants.

Position 2—The Crossing

Upright:
Forget MacGyver—your penchant for resourceful ideas far surpasses anything Hollywood could dream up. Your organizational skills aren't bad, either.

Reversed:
Your insecurity is making you hold everyone around you with a tighter grip than normal. Ease off the controlling behavior.

Position 3—The Base

Upright:
You are the Earth Mother, open, loving, and caring, a free spirit who loves deeply and is loved in return.

Reversed:
Money burns a hole in your pocket; you spend it faster than you make it. Clue: phone's ringing—it's for you.

Position 4—The Past

Upright:
Your hard working and practical, no-nonsense approach have helped you establish a solid foundation to build upon.

Reversed:
Snobby is as snobby does—they don't call you the material girl for nothing. Watch how you judge.

Position —The Crowning

Upright:
Staying within the lines is important to you. You take pride in how well everything runs when you are in charge.

Reversed:
Being a workaholic is a sure way to get into the early grave club. Take the advice you're being given.

Position 6—The Future

Upright:
Your attention to detail sets you apart from the competition and your experience level makes you the complete package.

Reversed:
Don't let shallow behavior cause you to miss out on something very important. There's more to life than money, you know.

Position 7—The Self

Upright:
You are practical and sensible. Not one to rock the boat, you prefer to maintain a low profile.

Reversed:
A little less sparkle and a little more substance, please. Broaden your circle of loved ones to include more than yourself.

Position 8 —Outside Influences

Upright:
With power comes responsibility; use yours wisely. You are naturally very protective of those you love and respect.

Reversed:
If you can't say anything nice, sit by me—that's your motto. Openly two-faced and courting gossip will not go unnoticed.

Position 9 —Hopes and Fears

Upright:
Your business instincts are right on target. Ignore the naysayers, follow your hunches, and watch everything fall into place.

Reversed:
A real friend is one who sticks by you no matter what. Fair-weather friends change with the climate. Which one are you?

Position 10 —The Outcome

Upright:
You are empathetic and compassionate, and able to see clearly to make the best choices for all concerned.

Reversed:
Pretentious and elitist, your entitled behavior has everyone shaking their heads. Have the good sense to be embarrassed about it.

The King of Pentacles

Captain of industry and finance, this "rags to riches" King is no stranger to hard work and doesn't believe in luck. He's ready to roll up his sleeves and get to work, but equally ready to enjoy the fruits of his labors.

Meaning in a Nutshell:
Achievement

Position 1—The Situation

Upright:
A true professional and dedicated to being at the top of your field, you don't let any worthy challenge slip by.

Reversed:
He who dies with the most toys wins—isn't that what you say? Less acquisition and more charity would do nicely.

Position 2

—The Crossing

Upright:
You don't make decisions hastily, but when you do, your judgment is sound. People watch you, then follow your lead.

Reversed:
You're not thinking things through and disaster is looming. Failure to plan today for the future could be your undoing.

Position 3—The Base

Upright:
Your education came from the school of hard knocks. Practical experience is more valuable than "book learning" in your opinion.

Reversed:
No matter how much you have, you still want more and more. Is there no end to your insatiable greed?

Position 4—The Past

Upright:
With the sound advice you were given, your investments were both wise and timely. You're now reaping the benefits of forethought.

Reversed:
Like it or not change is gonna happen, with or without you. Resisting it just makes the pain last that much longer.

Position
—The Crowning

Upright:
Slow to anger, you are benevolent and full of that parental unit confidence—no worries, you got this!

Reversed:
You judge others by who they know and what they can do for you, rather than who they really are.

Position 6—The Future

Upright:
Let common sense be your guide. It knows what is right for you and more importantly, what's right to do.

Reversed:
You use others to do your dirty work. Careful who you exploit, lest you end up on the receiving end.

Position 7—The Self

Upright:
Enterprising and inventive in your ambitions, take baby steps until it is time to take it to the next level.

Reversed:
Never one to miss telling an inappropriate joke, your idea of fun is rude, crude, and socially unacceptable. Clean up your act.

Position 8
—Outside Influences

Upright:
You are a highly valued and supportive team player, always ready with glowing compliments and stingy with unnecessary criticism.

Reversed:
The pangs of conscience don't seem to prickle as keenly as they used to. Your integrity isn't what it used to be.

Position 9
—Hopes and Fears

Upright:
Be cautious before you commit. Make sure your due diligence is complete, up to date, and to the letter.

Reversed:
You've got a ruthless streak that runs deep. Don't let your impatience write a check you're not willing to make good on.

Position 10
—The Outcome

Upright:
Wealthy and successful, your future is so bright you need shades. Oh, it's good to be the King!

Reversed:
You're so set on winning you want it at any cost. Consider what you're willing to give up before you risk it.

Conclusion

So you've completed the book—now what?

There are several paths before you, Grasshopper. You can decide to learn more or you can decide to stop here. Or you can set the book aside for now, go shoe shopping, and think about it tomorrow at Tara. You could even read a romance novel or two (I've got some recommendations… *nudge nudge wink wink*) The point is: it's all up to you how you proceed.

Hopefully, you've had a lot of fun reading through the interpretations. And I have a confession to make—in between all the fun and laughs, you've….um…actually been learning how to read the Tarot. Surprise! That's because hidden amongst the irreverent interpretations are the traditional, esoteric meanings behind the cards. And even if you can only remember the keywords at first, you're well on your way to becoming a proficient reader—and that is an EPIC WIN!

"In the universe, there are things that are known, and things that are unknown, and in between, there are doors."

—William Blake